186 Days in Teaching

186 Days in Teaching provides a month-by-month roadmap for the school year, helping secondary teachers quickly adapt to new environments, accomplish the many tasks expected of them and excel in roles that might be unfamiliar or outside their initial training.

The book covers all aspects of teaching and learning as well as non-teaching responsibilities, ensuring you know exactly what is coming up and how to prepare for it successfully. By offering practical advice, research-based strategies and evidence-informed approaches, this guide helps teachers navigate the annual cycle of school life while building the necessary skills and knowledge to remain adaptable and accelerate their careers. Key topics include retaining autonomy, curriculum design, pastoral care and effective communication. Drawing on well-known theories of community practice, it empowers teachers to become active agents in shaping their school's ethos and teaching practices.

With a focus throughout on your well-being and job satisfaction, this is essential reading for all secondary teachers, especially those new to the profession, aiming to build a fulfilling, sustainable career in a diverse education landscape.

James Shea leads the postgraduate and undergraduate teacher education courses as ITE portfolio leader in the School of Education at the University of Bedfordshire, UK. His research interests centre on the way memory is strengthened through the implementation of research such as retrieval practice.

Mohammed A. Amin is an experienced teacher educator and humanities lead tutor at the University of Bedfordshire, UK, who has worked in a range of educational settings. His research interests are centred on the development of teachers and the quality of mentoring for trainee teachers in secondary schools.

186 Days in Teaching

A Month-by-Month Guide to Being a Secondary Teacher

James Shea and Mohammed A. Amin

LONDON AND NEW YORK

Designed cover image: © Sarah Hoyle

First published 2026
by Routledge
4 Park Square, Milton Park, Abingdon, Oxon OX14 4RN

and by Routledge
605 Third Avenue, New York, NY 10158

Routledge is an imprint of the Taylor & Francis Group, an informa business

© 2026 James Shea and Mohammed A. Amin

The right of James Shea and Mohammed A. Amin to be identified as authors of this work has been asserted in accordance with sections 77 and 78 of the Copyright, Designs and Patents Act 1988.

All rights reserved. No part of this book may be reprinted or reproduced or utilised in any form or by any electronic, mechanical, or other means, now known or hereafter invented, including photocopying and recording, or in any information storage or retrieval system, without permission in writing from the publishers.

Trademark notice: Product or corporate names may be trademarks or registered trademarks, and are used only for identification and explanation without intent to infringe.

British Library Cataloguing-in-Publication Data
A catalogue record for this book is available from the British Library

Library of Congress Cataloging-in-Publication Data
Shea, James, 1970- author | Amin, Mohammed A. author
Title: 186 days in teaching : a month-by-month guide to being a secondary teacher / James Shea, Mohammed A. Amin.
Other titles: One hundred eighty-six days in teaching
Description: Abingdon, Oxon ; New York : Routledge, 2026. | Includes bibliographical references and index.
Identifiers: LCCN 2025014408 (print) | LCCN 2025014409 (ebook) | ISBN 9781032712208 hardback | ISBN 9781032712161 paperback | ISBN 9781032712178 ebook
Subjects: LCSH: Effective teaching | High school teaching | Mentoring in education
Classification: LCC LB1025.3 .S5273 2026 (print) | LCC LB1025.3 (ebook) | DDC 373.1102--dc23/eng/20250616
LC record available at https://lccn.loc.gov/2025014408
LC ebook record available at https://lccn.loc.gov/2025014409

ISBN: 978-1-032-71220-8 (hbk)
ISBN: 978-1-032-71216-1 (pbk)
ISBN: 978-1-032-71217-8 (ebk)

DOI: 10.4324/9781032712178

Typeset in Melior
by KnowledgeWorks Global Ltd.

Contents

186 days in teaching	1
September 20 days	5
October 15 days	12
November 20 days	39
December 15 days	50
January 18 days	61
February 18 days	67
March 20 days	77
April 10 days	86
May 20 days	94
June 15 days	101
July 13 days	108
August 2 days	113
And finally...	121
Index	123

186 days in teaching

Introduction

Summary

This introduction will introduce teachers to the wide panoply of schools, academies, trusts, federations and how they are seeking to centralise curriculum, policy and processes across their collections of institutions. It will set out the challenges of a teacher seeking to move within such institutions, as well as the toolset needed to ensure fluid employability. It will introduce the idea of how an assertive teacher can interact within the rules of fidelity to ensure they can affect the education being delivered and feel fulfilment in their role. It will broker the idea of transposable habitus and how this concept can enable teachers to move across the educational landscape and bolster their future employability and longevity within their careers.

School types and funding in England

The historical idea of schools in England being led by local councils and funded by a grant from central government to the local council has rapidly changed due to the marketisation of schools under successive Labour, coalition and Conservative governments. Schools can still be funded through the local council (known as grant maintained local authority schools) of which around 45% are still funded this way, but increasingly so they have an agreement with the Department for Education (DfE) in England which bypasses the council and instead establishes a direct relationship between the school and its Whitehall counterpart. Such schools are mainly known as academies and around 55% of schools are funded through a direct agreement, but there are some other types such as "free schools" (650 schools) and "University Technical Colleges" (UTCs) (44 schools). However, one of the main advantages of being a local authority school is having access to the backroom staff of human resources and other related services. To reproduce that advantage, academies, free schools and UTCs in England group together either loosely in the form of a federation, or legally, in the form of a trust, known as a Multi Academy Trust (MAT). As of 2025, there were around 1400 MATs made up of small to medium-sized MATs (2–11 schools) and around 130 large to super-large MATs (12–90 schools).

MATs are the dominant model for secondary schools in England

MATs are the dominant model in secondary education in England, but the rate of take-up in the primary sector is substantially lower with only four in ten primary schools being an academy in comparison to eight in ten secondary schools. This is because a small primary school is vulnerable to a falling intake and brings expensive risk to a MAT. As such, MATs are reluctant to take on primary schools. Furthermore, the governing boards of primary schools are also reluctant to lose the support and financial security of their local authority. As can be inferred from this reluctance, MATs are often run more on corporate lines with a clear eye on the balance sheet and reputation through national indicators such as GCSE results, league tables and the "Progress 8" measure (Progress 8 tells you about the progress that pupils in a school make from the end of primary school to the end of year 11).

Corporate style schools in MATs

To achieve consistency and presence within a market, MATs often attempt to have "their way" of doing things in the same way we see corporates achieve this in business. This "way" can be made up of tangibles such as uniforms, specific guidance around the presentation of learning materials and the layout of learning spaces, for example, the way tables are arranged. This "way" can also be non-tangibles such as pedagogical approaches, behaviour management strategies and the availability of curriculum options. What this means is that moving, as a teacher, from one MAT to another can mean a complete (corporate) culture shock. You might think you can redeploy your teaching expertise from one MAT to another quite readily, but if the contrast between MATs is too much you could find yourself making a poor start and unable to cope with the multitude of minutiae expected of you in order to be an effective teacher within the MAT. This risk is especially amplified if you are not an assertive teacher and simply accept that how things are done in your new MAT as the way things should be done. Whilst we do not suggest you go into your new school pointing out all of the things wrong in the way hundreds of teachers approach things or the pre-existing planning materials, we do suggest there is space for an intellectual and academic discussion to be had from a well-qualified and assertive teacher.

[Did you know there is an app called Teacher Tapp which asks 3 questions of teachers and school leaders every day? They publish the results of the survey the very next day alongside a helpful blog on an aspect of teaching or education. It's an excellent way to not only keep up to date with teaching but keep your finger on

the pulse of new and old educational initiatives in England and just what the teaching profession thinks about them! Go to www.teachertapp.co.uk to find out more.]

Teachers in England are well qualified

Around 80% of teachers in England will hold a postgraduate Level 7 qualification in teacher education in the form of a PGCE or PGDE and some will have taken that further and completed an MA. Indeed, a helpful Teacher Tapp survey shows 33% of teachers in England have a master's or a doctorate. The Frameworks for HE Qualifications of UK Degree-Awarding Bodies L7 descriptors set out carefully what such qualified people are able to do: "demonstrate self-direction and originality...act autonomously in planning and implementing tasks...initiative... decision-making in complex and unpredictable situations..." (QAA, 2014).

Tension between corporate MATs and well-qualified teachers

The problem comes when you prevent such a deeply qualified person from undertaking any of those things in the name of fidelity to the way a MAT had decided their teachers must approach the teaching of pupils within the MAT. Such qualities are valued across the country in sectors other than teaching and so if we don't take advantage of those qualities, if we don't enable teachers to participate in their institution and become part of the institution and help broker newcomers to the institution, then they are more likely to leave that school, that MAT and perhaps our profession. The world of work outside of teaching will happily consume potential employees with that level of qualifications, knowledge and skill set in today's competitive market.

Boosting employability through mobility

This book is not just a guide to working within secondary education schools within England; it is designed to help you move from one workplace to another and to ensure your career progresses in the direction you want to go. It will help you keep autonomy in your work, and it will also help you read the signs for when you need to move on to a new school or MAT. As much as we all like to stay in the same school for a long time, the reality is that for many teachers in England schools and MATs can change rapidly and it is quite possible the vast majority of teachers will need to move schools or MATs at one time of another in their careers.

Developing yourself for the unknown future school

Whether you are brand new to teacher training, an early career teacher, a teacher from overseas or indeed a well-established teacher there are some key things to consider when forging a career in schools within England and this book will helpfully go through all of these things. However, it would be wrong to see all schools as the same. How, then, does this book look to help you navigate these different schools, MATs, leaders and approaches to teaching, behaviour and so forth? By focusing on something known as transposable habitus. This is a term originally coined by Pierre Bourdieu, the French sociologist and it is a vital idea for teachers to grasp. Transposable knowledge, habits and skills combined equate to habitus. These ideas all explore a central theme, the unknown future. We build up cultural capital and a transposable habitus that enables us to be successful in different, unknown future areas of our lives. We accept, always, that there are limitations to these concepts of Bourdieu, but this concept of transposable habitus does have a place in education. What this means is that practice you learn in one school about how to teach does not automatically transpose into another school setting. This might be because you yourself reject the practice or it might be because your new school rejects or has no need for the practice. The sections on the "school ski trip" and "food parcels and extended pastoral care" are a good example of this. What might be an important set of skills and knowledge in one school might not be necessary in another. One school might think it important that every child in every year group, regardless of prior attainment, shows they are following the reading by holding a ruler on the text. You might object to this idea as it is a reading strategy for weaker readers and applying it to every child doesn't seem a sensible use of a support strategy. In moving to another school where this practice isn't used you might dispose of this practice and revert to recommending it to weaker readers to help them follow the text. Indeed, an assertive teacher in a healthy school might raise in a departmental meeting to know what academic literature the policy was based upon and offer up academic literature to the contrary. The same assertive teacher might be more interested in knowing when the deadline for resignations is! This book enables you to evaluate your school and know if you need to engage in a critical debate or move on to a more agreeable school environment. A happy teacher stays in their school for a long time and once you have found the right school for you, outcomes for your pupils will rise for them as well as for you! We hope you enjoy this book and find it helpful to dip into or read month by month as you go through the different stages of a new school. Even if you are an experienced teacher, moving schools can be quite a change in culture and this book will help you make that positive start that ensures your new school values you and the contributions you can make to the school community.

[The National Foundation for Educational Research is an independent body which seeks to evaluate data within the teaching profession to provide insights into examinations, pupils, teachers, leaders and other statistics. It releases regular blogs and publications and is most helpful for any teacher seeking to view information about teaching and schools in England. You can sign up for their regular newsletter at https://www.nfer.ac.uk]

September 20 days

Introduction

September is all about getting off to a strong start with new classes. This chapter focuses on planning for new classes and early behaviour management. It covers how to quickly adapt to a school's culture, makes a strong first impression and establishes key expectations for behaviour management. You will find advice on onboarding sessions, understanding school policies and building rapport with pupils. Practical tips on accessing pupil information through databases, SENCO, Pastoral Leads and previous teachers are also included to help you hit the ground running.

Planning for new classes and early behaviour management

This section will discuss how the school's culture helps new teachers adapt quickly and make a strong first impression. It covers onboarding sessions on behaviour management, school values, safeguarding and organisational systems. Key expectations for behaviour management and first lessons will be outlined, advising on establishing expectations and building rapport. Teachers will learn to consider pupils' needs and present new units effectively. The chapter will also explain school policies on behaviour, mobile phones, uniforms and equipment, and stress the importance of understanding pupils' backgrounds for planning. Practical advice on accessing pupil information through databases, SENCO, Pastoral Lead and previous teachers will be provided.

Meeting your pupils

September in any school year often sees staff meeting pupils for the first time, both as pastoral figures and as subject teachers. For some pupils, this will also be their first introduction to the school's ethos, approach to teaching, learning and behaviour. This is particularly common in secondary school entry years, such as Year 7 for 11-year-olds or Year 9 for 13-year-olds (as in some Upper Schools in

England are 13–18), depending on the region. While you, as a new teacher, might also be adjusting to the school environment, pupils will likely perceive you as an experienced member of staff. Adopting this confident stance is crucial. A strong grasp of the school's behaviour management policy, including its strictness and procedural guidelines for rule infractions, is essential. Additionally, understanding the pastoral context of individual pupils can make a significant difference. For example, a pupil may be dealing with challenging personal circumstances, such as spending weekends with an alcoholic parent, which could affect their preparedness for school e.g., on a Monday, frequently missing essential PE clothing or they might not always have done their homework. Consulting a pupil's personal data on the school system before initiating major disciplinary actions can ensure that your response aligns with a broader, collaborative approach taken by all staff interacting with the pupil. This doesn't mean bypassing policies but ensuring that actions are informed and part of a unified strategy.

Schools increasingly rely on electronic systems to support communication and information sharing. As a new teacher, you will likely use central databases to access a pupil's SEND requirements, pastoral records, attendance History and more. Familiarity with these tools will enable you to stay informed and make data-driven decisions that benefit both your teaching practice and your pupils' learning experiences.

Reviewing prior learning of examination content

This section sets out how teachers need to review learning against exam board requirements and review prior learning. It will articulate and advise on how to review the examinations that pupils are undertaking, the coverage of their exam content from the previous year and the need.

Knowing the exam criteria

Pupils will do better if they understand the journey they are on and can piece together knowledge and skills, as well as using articulate English to show competence in an exam. Even if done to a lesser degree, this makes reviewing prior knowledge against exam criteria more effective. Whilst it is important that you teach beyond an examination, if you are taking a GCSE or A-level class, then it is vital you cover the assessment objectives from the specification as well as ensure that your pupils are familiar with the language of the questions they will face.

Make sure that all knowledge taught in lessons is assessed and revisited. There is nothing to gain for pupils or teachers if the questions cannot be answered. Allocate sufficient time to revisit key knowledge, whether as a homework task or ten minutes at the end of the lesson. Without this, pupils will rapidly forget what they have learned or not be able to align it within their mental schemata for that topic.

Both pupil and teacher should use the review of learned materials to improve themselves, the teacher as a practitioner and the pupil as a learner. If pupils are made aware of how a specific skillset enhances their knowledge base and aligns with exam criteria, this fosters independent thinking and metacognition, which, as teachers, we know may be elusive for some pupils but can be a watershed moment for pupils' academic and independent development.

Know your assessment objectives

Different knowledge and skills are required for different questions depending on the assessment objectives from the specification being assessed or developed. Even if it is a Key Stage 3 class, you will still be developing foundational knowledge and ideas so that they progress well into Key Stage 4. For example, an 8-mark question comparing sources in History or data in Geography requires different skills than a 4-mark question on a diagram in Science. Pupils need to know what is being assessed generally, as well as what the answers are to questions. Assess how well these skills have been learned and practised by pupils when they go to answer a specific question on a topic area. Build meaningful assessments into lessons so that the familiarity of questions, structure and time pressures are less daunting. For example, plan five or ten minutes at regular points for assessment, such as one exam question every four lessons. If you do not see this in your centralised planning, raise this with the head of department and explain that you are going to insert some sequential examination question development into the planning.

Analyse performance and reteach misconceptions

Conduct regular data analysis to inform what has been learned well and what needs improvement. For example, in Geography, if pupils confuse the ring of fire with fault lines in a diagram question, adapt your centralised planning to address these misconceptions. Adapting planning to reflect learning misconceptions is vital. There are many ways to do this, such as revisiting specific topics or using different teaching methods to clarify misunderstandings. Do not be so rigid to centralised planning that you cannot stop and reteach something if you feel many in the class are not confident in a key topic area. Misconceptions lead to substantial learning issues and so it is vital that they are removed from schemata, by the pupils, as soon as possible.

Reviewing pre-existing curriculum design

This section sets out approaches to ensure curriculum design is evidence-informed and up-to-date. It will cover an overview of how to review existing curriculum materials and adapt them depending on the learning needs of the cohort.

Autonomy or restriction?

It could be you have come from a school where you were allowed considerable freedom to plan and design your own individual lessons. You may have had the freedom to create resources for projection onto a screen or an interactive whiteboard along with classroom-based resources. This approach to self-planning by teachers has rapidly been receding as schools within England have adapted to the economies of scale afforded by being in groups of schools – whether as a trust or as a federation. It may well be that you still enjoy and value the freedom to plan your own lessons to your own specific design, but that value will likely reduce your employability and ability to move from area to area and from school to school. The approach taken by many secondary schools in England is to have a centralised curriculum. One that has been designed by in-house subject experts and which fits the values and approaches of the group of schools that will be using the curriculum. Upon entering the school you might find materials for screen and desk all centrally produced and seemingly no space for your creative lesson planning.

Whilst some will lament the loss of this autonomy, there will be many who welcome this change in practice. Learning how to plan from scratch whilst being a trainee teacher was pushing lots of prospective teachers out of the profession as they failed to cope with the workload of writing all their planning and being a novice lesson planner at the same time. In a world of well-being and workload-friendly practice, having pre-existing planning in place for teachers is seen as a good thing. It frees up time for teachers to spend more time with their families and enjoy their lives. However, at the same time, it has been recognised that removing all autonomy for planning from teachers leaves them feeling disenfranchised and disillusioned. Indeed, these teachers often also want to quit teaching. So, what is the answer to keep you in our profession?

Having the freedom to adapt pre-existing planning is clearly the answer and a midpoint between the two approaches. But before you rush off and start adapting those carefully curated and written plans, be aware – central and senior leaders are often not keen on you adapting their expensively produced curriculums. However, they are experienced teachers themselves and understand the notion of evidence-informed practice. Here is where you can ensure that you can adapt pre-existing planning and ensure that senior leaders approve of your adaptations.

Scenario 1 – A topic selected is not cultivating epistemic curiosity

Imagine you have taught the pre-existing planning for this topic once before and it is clear it is counterproductive to your teaching. The planning is pedestrian; it clearly delivers the minimum knowledge and uses basic study techniques, such as repetitive quizzes, to ensure the pupils learn the knowledge required to progress, but pupils complain that the topic is dull and irrelevant and the teaching uninspiring.

You decide you wish to make a change to the teaching, but before you start doing so, you have to take on board that the school or multi-academy trust (MAT) has commissioned this planning and will be resistant to a new teacher coming in and making changes. However, as a central theme of this book argues, you are in a position to push for changes so long as you have good evidence to back up your proposals for change.

Answer 1 – What evidence do you have to present?

A paper published by Dubey, Griffiths and Lombrozo (2022) titled *If it's important, then I'm curious: Increasing perceived usefulness stimulates curiosity* offers a clear route to pushing for adaptation of the pre-existing curriculum. The paper suggests you "consider stimulating curiosity by changing the perceived usefulness of a scientific topic" (pp. 1–2). Their results were clear, "both personal and social usefulness were positive and significant predictors of curiosity" (p. 2).

With this evidence, you are in a position to offer to adapt the pre-existing planning so that personal and social usefulness of the topic are highlighted through a range of techniques designed to stimulate curiosity. A sensible approach would be to adapt the pre-existing planning for one or two lessons as a "sample" and then send the adapted sample along with the paper to your head of department or senior school leader in charge of curriculum. Offer to "pilot" changing the planning for the topic based on the new evidence and that you would also use pupil voice to find out whether the planning is delivering the new intended outcome of increased curiosity. The advantage of this approach is that it mirrors the tools that teachers who undertake research as part of a PGCE, a PGDE or a master's in education would use. This increasing use of academic tools to cultivate strong evidence to provide a mandate for change is what this book is proposing to all teachers. Evidence-informed teachers will enjoy greater autonomy over their teaching role and be in a better place to stay in the profession.

Building rapport with new pupils and colleagues

This section focuses on how to create a professional relationship with pupils that will last the time they are in school. It will set out how to establish professional relationships with pupils and other members of staff, which is important to achieve, and that using humour and being flexible in dealing with issues will help develop those positive relationships. It will look to help you plan for the long term as these pupils will be with you for up to six more years!

Multitudinous pupils!

As a teacher of 120–150 pupils a day (if you base a teaching day on 5 lessons a day with an average of 25–30 pupils in each class), you will be one of up to 5 different teachers that will teach a pupil in a day with an average of 25 lessons a week. You will meet them, and they may see you as one of many teachers that will teach them in that year at school, but more broadly, you may be one of 10 to 30 teachers they may have had during their schooling experience up till that point. Some of your pupils may not like school. Some of them may hate teachers, but you have to believe that you will be the one who makes school worth the journey, the bus ride and the issues, as you build a positive rapport with them.

When meeting them for the first time, simple actions, like being positive in how you engage with them, allow the ones that liked their previous teachers to think that you are going to be another excellent teacher in their lives. It makes the reluctant learners want to come to your lessons because they have high expectations of you as a teacher. In effect, you have built a contract with the pupil with your high standards and their high expectations. This is where centralised planning can be helpful. Instead of being time-poor and having to work hard on creating resources from scratch, instead, you can be adapting the planning and resources to your pupils and their specific needs.

Be prepared

Being prepared with the PowerPoint, any paper-based resources and the SEND adaptions shows your pupils that you have high standards around organisation. What they really like is when you attempt to know the names of your pupils. Names matter in building positive relations and pupils will not mind that you have a printout of their pictures and names and use it to help you same precise pupils' names when undertaking targeted questioning. An organised teacher who effortlessly navigates their resources, manages their timings and who rapidly learns their pupils' names is the sort of teacher pupils want to have teaching them. Be that prepared teacher and you will find the pupils will respond accordingly.

Be confident

Positive body language by standing upright, having confident eye contact and gaze and regular scanning of the room for rule infractions is what pupils expect from high-performing teachers in England. Avoid being behind the desk, even if you feel nervous and be the leader of the room, drama studio or playing field. Some new pupils may be nervous in school and you can help them by being confident. Being a teacher that is firm and friendly rather than hostile will make a big difference, especially for pupils who may not have had positive experiences with your predecessor or current colleagues. Affirming that you intend to use the behaviour policy with rewards, as well as the sanctions, deployed for an effort that any pupils can achieve will also show that you plan to highlight achievement. If you reward things that only a few pupils can achieve you will sow disaffection amongst the remainder. Reward them for things you want to see – getting their things out promptly, being first to start a task, offering to help distribute resources and working well as a pair. All these things create a culture of positive performance for a confident teacher.

Reference

Dubey, R., Griffiths, T. L., & Lombrozo, T. (2022). If it's important, then I'm curious: Increasing perceived usefulness stimulates curiosity. *Cognition, 226*, pp. 1–7.

October 15 days

Introduction

In October, the focus shifts to using the school's behaviour management policy to establish authority. This chapter explains how to effectively promote a productive learning environment by understanding and implementing the behaviour management policy. It covers when and how to hand out sanctions safely, the importance of consistency and how to work with the wider pastoral team and parents. The goal is to empower teachers to teach effectively while maintaining positive relationships with pupils.

Using the school's behaviour management policy to establish authority

This section sets out how to step up the use of a behaviour management policy when classes begin to struggle to continue high standards of behaviour after a good start to term. It will explain how to understand the behaviour management policy effectively to promote a fruitful environment where pupils can learn when to hand out sanctions and how to do so in a safe way. It will cover pastoral areas such as how to work with wider members of the pastoral team, such as the head of house/year and with parents. It will explain the importance of avoiding the pitfall of copying other members of staff as they will have gained capital through their own experiences with the pupils and their own interpretations of behaviour management policy. It will explore how policies may differ across schools and how implementation of similar policies like that of phones or trainers may vary, as well as how to use the behaviour management policy as a way to empower teachers to teach, avoiding forging poor relationships with pupils. It will conclude with the importance of online reporting mechanisms, thus creating a trail of evidence of how one manages problematic pupils.

DOI: 10.4324/9781032712178-3

Consistency rules!

As secondary school teachers in England, maintaining high standards of behaviour throughout the term can be challenging because, after a while of teaching your class, you will begin to develop good relationships with your pupils. This, conversely, makes it harder to sanction a hardworking and well-behaved pupil for an occasional misdemeanour, and you can be tempted to let it go. Whilst for one hardworking and self-regulated pupil this could well be the right decision, the issue is when you apply this new rule to the entire class. A less hardworking pupil who is not so self-regulated will often rely on the external motivation of avoiding sanctions to comply with high expectations around behaviour. Thus, what might seem like a reasonable piece of leniency to one pupil is actually detrimental to the entire class and their motivation to behave. If a class sees that you are consistent across the class, even with those who are generally well-behaved and effectively self-regulated, then they will respect you and your implementation of the school behaviour management policy more readily. They need you to be fair and consistent with your behaviour management, regardless of who it is.

Something to consider embedding into your behaviour management policy is explaining "the why" of good behaviour. There is an approach to behaviour which is founded on the principles of "behaviour for learning." That is behaviour which improves the learning of individuals, pairs, groups or the whole class. Simple things like having the correct equipment or being prompt to begin work at the start of an activity deliver easy learning gains. Having a meta-narrative with your pupils, which explains how the rules you are implementing in the classroom are helping them to learn, reduces levels of defiance. Do not tell everyone just to stop talking; tell them to stop talking so that everyone can hear the instructions clearly.

School-led behaviour management policies

A fundamental principle of behaviour management in English schools is that the school leadership will set the behaviour management policy for all teachers and all classrooms. The very first thing you must do when beginning work in a school is to review the behaviour management policy and ensure that you react in exactly the way it sets out. This is linked to both promoting good behaviour and also to safeguarding. A school must be confident that all professionals on its premises will approach situations where behaviour by a pupil brings risk to themselves or others in a consistent way. Inconsistency not only undermines the behaviourist approach of a school to ensure all pupils embrace behaviour for learning, but it can also lead to safeguarding issues. Keeping children safe is a non-negotiable priority for schools, and their behaviour management policy will be closely linked to this. You should ensure you study key trigger points where you are expected to call upon centralised services and support to ensure that the children in your care enjoy consistent expectations and actions from you when their behaviour presents a risk to their learning or well-being or the learning and well-being of others.

One thing to consider with a behaviour management policy is what it is trying to achieve. It wants to deliver an environment to both pupils and teachers that enables all to thrive academically and socially. Secondary school is where pupils turn from children into adults, and as secondary teachers, we want to ensure that they can do that safely and responsibly. Whether you are teaching your own subject, are in charge of a form class or leading a personal and social education lesson, it is important that pupils feel they are encouraged to both learn and interact in a way that prepares them for adulthood, further or higher education, work and being a responsible member of society. As such, it is up to the collective group of teachers and leaders within the school (and sometimes staff from the MAT) who come together around a central behaviour management policy. The policy has to deliver both a positive teaching AND a positive learning atmosphere. Staff and pupils need to both feel that they can work together in all aspects of the school (e.g., during extra-curricular activities, not just during lesson time) in a way that delivers a positive and productive atmosphere.

A critical part of successfully creating and delivering this positive and productive atmosphere will not be about managing high-profile and unusual behavioural incidents. These are likely to be managed by experienced staff as part of a long-running and ongoing intervention strategy. Rather, it will be mainstream teachers being attuned to variables such as declining engagement, an increase in disruptive behaviour or poor interactions between a pupil and one or more of their peers. Looking out for these signs and taking early and consistent, but supportive action is as critical to a school's behaviour management as it is to dealing with unusual and critical incidents.

Sanctions and rewards

The first thing to consider is the use of sanctions and rewards. These are the lifeblood of the low-stakes, "nudge" style tactics that teachers can use to ensure pupils are following the rules of the behaviour management policy and working hard during their lessons.

Teachers should be taking advantage of rewards and understanding their role in creating a positive and productive atmosphere. What you reward is what you want to see. A pupil arrives promptly, sits down, gets their coat off and their equipment out and sets about their first task immediately is what any teacher wants to see. So, reward this behaviour frequently. You set your pupils off on a short think, pair, share activity and two pupils immediately talk constructively and make notes ready to feed back to the whole class. You should reward this. Do not fall into the trap of focusing solely on negative behaviour and issuing sanctions for what you think pupils are not doing. You should be seen as a fair person, ready to issue rewards for something that any pupil could do. If you only reward pupils for things which only some pupils can achieve (a high standard of attainment, for example), then only pupils who can attain the reward will be motivated by it.

Having said that, a firm and consistent teacher who picks up low-level behaviour quickly and deals with it promptly will be one who has prevented poor behaviour from escalating into severely poor behaviour.

It is important to understand that each school or Multi Academy Trust (MAT) will be unique in what freedom you have to exercise discretion over the use of sanctions for transgressions of the behaviour management policy. Some schools have zero tolerance, and, as such, if the rule is that pupils do not talk in the corridor and a pupil says "good morning" to you in the corridor, then you would sanction them. It is likely the pupil knows they are not to talk in the silent corridor and is testing your boundaries, so if you are in this kind of school, be sure to follow through and issue sanctions as the school policy expect you to.

Some schools will have two policies. One informal policy that is up to teachers, and one that is formal and preceded by warnings. For example, a pupil might tip their chair up or lean their head on their hand, and you would issue a warning rather than a sanction. Should the behaviour continue, you would then escalate it to the next level of the behaviour management policy. This could be as informal as putting their name on the board or as formal as entering something into a computer system which tracks poor behaviour.

It is important to note that even the nature of sanctions varies from school to school. In some schools, there are centralised detentions. You enter the detention into a school's system, and that is the end of your involvement. Someone else contacts the parents, informs the pupil, supervises the sanction and sets work for during the sanction. In other schools, you are expected to communicate with the parents and the pupil, supervise the detention and set work for the pupil. This latter system will mean you should consult with someone experienced to ensure that how you communicate, what you say and how you supervise the detention is undertaken in a way that is similar to how an experienced member of staff would undertake the process.

As you can see, behaviour management varies from school to school and from MAT to MAT, and further, it is a team effort. It requires senior leaders, pastoral teams and individual subject teachers all working together collaboratively to deliver a holistic approach to ensuring high standards of behaviour that leads to a good learning environment which is supportive and pastorally safe. Teachers cannot shy away from sanctioning pupils, but they should also reward that which all pupils are able to achieve.

School pastoral system

One critical thing for any new member of staff, whether fresh from teacher training or moving from one school to another, is to learn about the school's pastoral system. You should identify who the leaders of houses, years and teams are and be sure to consult with them as you begin to interact with those in the school who have more regular contact with the pastoral system. This means where there are nuances to be had, your work reflects that knowledge the pastoral team has, and further, your work reinforces the relationships the pastoral team have built up with the families and carers of those pupils they interact with more than others.

One powerful factor behind behaviour management in any school will be the parents or guardians of the children you teach and their involvement with the child's behaviour. Whatever a parent or guardian's involvement is like, having a positive relationship with them and fostering open communication will ensure that when a child becomes involved with the behaviour management process, you can maximise its effect. Parents and guardians, in the main, want their child to do well in school, to feel supported – challenged even, and to be happy. They are often prepared to invest considerable time and effort into this. It is important not to judge parents by the behaviour of their child. Some children with substantive behavioural difficulties can have very invested parents or guardians, whilst at the same time, a child with no behavioural difficulties could just as well have parents who have little interest in their child's progression within school. Having said that, when a parent selects a school for their child, they are in effect agreeing to the school's behaviour management policy alongside the school's values and vision. Some schools go so far as to ask parents to sign a contract agreeing to support the school before the child begins their education at the school. That premise is where it is important – that school staff and parents are joint allies in reinforcing behavioural expectations. This goes for both school and at home – with parents expected to ensure their children have sufficient sleep, engage with set homework and attend events designed to bring parents and school staff together around the child, such as parents' evenings or open evenings.

Contacting parents about behaviour

It may be that your school has signed a contract with an Information and Communication Technology (ICT) provider to empower parent and school communications. These can be as simple as automated emails or text messages when a child is absent from school. Or they can be complex and powerful app-based software solutions, which enable parents to receive and access considerable data about a child's behaviour in school. There has to be a word of caution as one parent reported being inundated with automated one-way communications during a particularly challenging week for their child. There was no way for the parent to communicate back with the school via the app, as the communications were sent from a donotreply@ email box. In the main, however, you should expect to be quickly onboarded by Human Resources (HR) into the software used to communicate with parents, but you would be well advised to put aside ten minutes with an experienced colleague to identify the limitations of the software and any issues you should be aware of when using the software to communicate with parents about their child's behaviour. Whether communication is quite traditional or your school is signed up to the most contemporary cloud-based communication software, you should not lose sight of the guiding principles of parent and school communication. The collaborative nature of these discussions is always focused on finding solutions that benefit the pupil's overall development, whether a child is receiving negative behaviour from others or whether their behaviour is detrimental to their development or other pupils' development.

One thing that you can do is to recognise the fact that you are bringing with you a whole range of unique experiences and perspectives from your life, education and training events into your world of teaching. This includes your experiences in managing the behaviour of children and the types of behaviour that you have observed. You may have seen others, in the past, using strategies successfully to deal with a situation and be keen to deploy such a strategy yourself. However, it is important to pause and reflect on the unique nature of your school and individual classes. Each school, class and child will be different, and the strategies and methods which inspire them to exhibit the self-control and behaviour for learning needed to succeed in school will also vary. There is nothing wrong with having experience, but it is as limiting as it is enabling. Having the humility to not adopt a position of hubris when it comes to behaviour management will enable you to learn from your school and peers about how that particular school's cohorts are best inspired and managed. You should be thinking about adapting and personalising your strategies to the specific context of your school.

Reflective teachers

Remember, behaviour management policies will and do vary from school to school and from trust to trust. Even within a school and from department to department, you will see nuanced differences. Understanding these variations in policy and practice is the key to being strong at behaviour management. If you find yourself issuing 17 after-school detentions for one class in one lesson, then something has gone wrong somewhere, and the answer was not 17 after-school detentions! Behaviour management, whether trust, school or department, will be socially constructed and rely on that social construction. The policy is but a plan; the reality is the practice on the ground. A school will expect you to be as aware of the intrinsic and extrinsic reward policy as much as the sanctions policy. They will want you to foster a positive and inspiring learning environment, and they will expect you to maintain order for learning and keep staff and pupils safe. Reflect and consider: you should be doing as many positive telephone calls home as you are doing negative telephone calls.

Relationships and behaviour management

This brings us to the next stage of behaviour management – the quality of your relationships with your pupils. Relationships need to be built, as well as trust and respect earned. Having consistent, high-quality behaviour is a strong way to build such trust. But it has to be consistent. For example, if you never ask your pupils to work in silence, then do not be surprised if they find it difficult to do when you finally do ask them to do so. Ensuring your lessons regularly include periods of silent work conditions for your pupils to know that when you want them to work in silence, you mean they have to work in silence. If a class is not used to working in silence, then you should start with short periods of silent working, preceded by some kind of paired talking activity. This will enable you to answer any clarification questions and allow the pupils to try out their ideas on their designated partner before attempting to undertake the silent work. From there, you will be able to extend the length of time your pupils are used to working in silence until it is a strong part of your practice, and the pupils have good self-management of their work during such periods. If you go all out for long periods of silent working with a class who do not have a culture of silent working, then you will find it hard to establish a relationship with your pupils because you will be sanctioning them frequently in order to ensure they are on task. Building the silent work slowly, using praise and reward along with controlled paired talking prior to undertaking silent work, will enable pupils to feel proud of themselves for being able to sustain their work and to recognise that you have made it possible. It could be that your pupils are used to silent work and readily undertake this, but you should never assume this and should gently and positively build the length of silent work as quickly as possible.

Pupils enjoy working well for high-quality teachers – that is something that is important to understand. Traditionally, parents would be unaware of the day-to-day successes of their children and have to rely on formal reporting functions such as parents' evenings or reports. In today's modern and technologically advanced world, online reporting can enhance the communication and relationship between parents, pupils and teachers. You should set out from the start to build this relationship using such digital reportage tools to help create a trail of evidence that you, the pupil and the parents can reflect on during the parents' evening. Ensure you are fully conversant with not just the mechanics of how such digital tools are used but also how your peers are using the tools to report to parents. This will ensure that what you are doing is similar to what other teachers in your school are doing, and thus parents and pupils can expect high and consistent standards in how you are providing the information about either a pupil's successes or, as sometimes is necessary, their shortcomings.

This is not to conflate the regular online reporting mechanisms with the need to document incidents related to more serious matters. These include safeguarding, racism and any incidents which could be in contravention of the 2010 Equality

Act and the protected characteristics. Your school will have a very specific set of procedures for the reporting and escalation of incidents related to these more serious themes and you should ensure that you follow these procedures explicitly. If you are a teacher from another country, then you might not be used to some of the legislation which governs schools in England and so it is important to be aware of how formal guidance or legislation like the 2010 Equality Act or the *Keeping Children Safe in Education* Guidance strictly control how schools are managed and the way they respond to and report incidents.

Liaising with colleagues

This section sets out appropriate approaches to creating strong professional relationships with important teachers and middle or senior leaders within any secondary school. It covers how working in any new organisation is challenging and in teaching where the focus is on working as part of a community of practice, with each pupil having been seen and taught by between 6 and 12 people a day how cooperation is essential. It will set out how the skills of communication and using one's talents are vital, and how there are often nuances that may be misunderstood, such as the tone of an email, the words used in a casual conversation in the corridor or whose milk is used by whom in the staff room.

Leadership in schools

Although schools in England may present themselves as being hierarchical with Multi Academy Trusts having chief operating officers (CEOs) above Heads of School (not to be confused with a headteacher who has more autonomy), a school senior leadership team (SLT) which in turn is above a middle leadership (ML) all focused on leading the teaching workforce – the reality is that everyone works together as a team. Without high-quality collaboration and professionalism in the relationships between the various teachers, regardless of seniority, the institution will not be able to build an effective educational environment. This chapter provides a comprehensive guide on how to build and maintain these relationships, emphasising the importance of cooperation and communication in a school setting where each secondary pupil interacts with multiple teachers on a daily basis.

Values-led approaches

One set of values that underpins how successful schools operate is to ensure that approaches to relationships across the school are built on trust, respect and collaboration. If the educational community within a school, which is made up of a wide range of professional staff as well as teachers, is to be cohesive, then values which foster relationships are the way to make this happen.

The first approach that helps develop this value is the notion of active listening. This means when someone in a school community communicates with you, you acknowledge the substantive content of the message. This can be in the form of emails, whereby you might summarise some key messages from their email in your reply. It could be in the form of oral communication, whether that is face-to-face or online. Visibly making notes and ensuring that you are on message with what has been communicated to you really fosters a culture of respect. Seeing someone write down a point you have made makes the person communicating feel their point has been heard. Being a secondary teacher can mean you can be almost chaotically busy, moving from class to class and meeting to meeting. It can be a day or two before you get a chance to reflect on what someone said to you, and having taken good notes at the time is critical for being able to respond in a professional and organised way.

The next approach to consider is how often you have dialogue with your colleagues. There will be some natural opportunities through formal meetings, but they usually have quite a precise agenda, and it is unlikely that you will have extra time to undertake activities specific to an agenda of your own. One way that many schools try to foster regular collaboration is through professional learning communities (PLCs). These can exist within the school, or if the school is in a trust, they can exist across multiple schools. These professional communities are often themed and tend to be more collaborative and experimental rather than focused on day-to-day business-like traditional school meetings.

Getting the most from your personal learning community

There are usually core themes to PLCs, and they will be related to key areas within the school. A typical example would be teaching and learning within a professional development programme. Teachers across a MAT or a school will have issues or interests that transcend subjects. These are often focused on things like demographics (e.g., boys and reading), examinations (e.g., booster sessions), well-being and inclusion (e.g., LGBTQ inclusion) or even developmental Educational Psychology (e.g., remembering more). One of the key aspects of this book is that autonomy in the modern English school is earned by being evidence-informed and engaged in academic discussions, which lead to policy and practice. Unless you participate in PLCs, you will find your voice is marginalised from policy and practice, which emerges from these groups and is instigated and encouraged through policy, professional development and coaching. It is essential to see PLCs as opportunities to inform and influence your MAT and school and to ensure that the practice which emerges is of a high standard and well-informed.

Even within subject areas, with fixed agendas, there will be areas where you can collaborate with your colleagues and inform policy and practice. Each subject area will need to have specific planning and teaching strategies, which will include ensuring that some form of pre-existing planning is in place for teachers. This can vary hugely depending on school and department. One department may have slide decks which teachers can adapt to suit their classes, whereas another department may have pre-printed booklets for which no autonomy is allowed in terms of editing. However, all departments will engage in medium to long-term review and rewriting of planning and teaching materials. This discussion of planning and teaching will take place during departmental meetings and be informed by more than just anecdotal sources. It might be that you have read a primary research paper or a secondary book which suggests new ways to approach the planning and teaching of children in your subject area. It may well be that a new topic within your subject area has emerged, and you feel that the curriculum needs to be better diversified in order to ensure that the new topic area is included. Alternatively, you might have taught a particular topic, slide deck or booklet and found that some or all of the children in your class did not make expected progress or found it hard to remember key information or skills from the topic area. This is an opportunity for you to step up and offer to either edit pre-existing planning and teaching resources or to write a whole new set of planning and teaching resources from scratch. Secondary school departments in England run or fail on collaborative colleagues. Either there is a top-down imposed set of planning and teaching resources or the department works together to adapt and refine the pre-existing materials to ensure they are best suited to the pupils in their school. It is your responsibility to step up and collaborate with your colleagues to help deliver high-quality teaching and learning through well-informed planning and teaching materials.

It is important to understand that secondary departments in England are usually made up of more than one teacher. There are exceptions in some schools where there is simply a single music or drama teacher, but even then, they will be collaborating with colleagues in similar departments. This means that the department will co-construct its subject identity. Within the department, a reciprocal validation of knowledge will take place. Just like at university, each subject specialist will have topic areas within a subject where they have far greater knowledge than the rest of the department. For example, one English teacher will know a great deal about Gothic literature, whereas another will have detailed knowledge of post-war American drama. Collectively, a department will have various strengths across the department and blend these together to help curate a strong department where colleagues can collaborate, share knowledge and validate each other's specialist topic areas within a subject. As a new member of the department, you should work hard to discover which teachers are experts in certain topic areas, but also ensure that they are aware of where you can contribute specialist knowledge from your own areas of subject knowledge. Expressing appreciation and validation of specialist topic knowledge within your colleagues can significantly strengthen your collective professional relationships and ensure the department is strong and successful.

Such collaboration will only be successful if you are prepared to ask for assistance and help as part of a collaborative department. There is no escaping that you will be exceptionally busy, with very few spare minutes during any working day. Indeed, in a secondary school in England, it will not just be colleagues popping into your room at break, lunchtime, before or after school – it will be your pupils! Yet, when a member of your department asks you for some help, it is critical that you put aside some time to give them your attention and knowledge and ensure that their work is supported by your assistance. This reciprocal approach fosters a sense of community and shared responsibility.

Constructive feedback

It is likely that when entering a new school, you enter a new professional development environment. Each MAT or school will have its own specific way of doing this. Some schools or MATs will have appointed a senior leader to run the professional development programme and to put into place systems and processes to ensure that teachers are developing within their subject-specific departments. This will mean it is highly likely your head of department, as well as other colleagues within the department, will be providing you with feedback as part of this process. Indeed, it is also highly likely that you will be providing as well as receiving constructive feedback, as this is an integral part of professional development. The type of feedback and coaching you offer will depend on the professional development model that the school or MAT has embraced. It could be prescriptive instructional coaching where you or a colleague is asked to keep to a precise script during a teaching episode. It could also be co-constructed instructional coaching where you and your colleague co-construct the target and then work together to help develop the area of teaching to be enhanced. Whichever approach you use, you will need to see that being open to feedback from a colleague and seeing the feedback as an opportunity for development is essential for a successful and collaborative department.

The challenge of working in a new organisation

As you will see, from all the areas that are required as part of working as a collaborative department, being part of a new organisation, whether that is as a department, a school or a MAT, means adapting to new systems, processes and established ways of working as part of a community of practice. You will not just be teaching your pupils, you will be liaising with multiple other teachers on a daily basis, meaning that cooperation is essential to high standards. Therefore, you will have to accept that your previous experience may not transfer as easily as you might have expected. The school culture from which you have recently left prior to taking your new position will be substantially different in its values, traditions and norms. Understanding the difference between the old culture and the new culture is crucial for you as a new teacher. Integral to this will be the decision-making and lines of accountability. These are also likely to be substantially different from school to school. Understanding who (or whether) to approach someone before undertaking something in your new school is essential. In some schools, you might be expected to organise trips for your pupils. Rather than asking permission to undertake the trip, you would instead consult others such as the safeguarding lead or examinations officer with the assumption that organising trips is a good thing. In other schools, you might be expected to obtain permission from a specific person who would evaluate whether your trip is educationally worthwhile. Indeed, some schools eschew trips altogether in the pursuit of grades. Understanding the new norms in your new school is essential if you are to work collaboratively and understand how to network and negotiate within the cultural norms.

One thing you can expect as a new member of staff is an on-boarding programme of study. It is in a school's interest to ensure new members of staff understand key policies, procedures and expectations and so these programmes, often put into place by Human Resources and delivered by experienced members of staff, will be offered to you so that you can acclimatise quickly and effectively to your new school. The high-stakes areas such as safeguarding and behaviour management will both feature early on. Although you will have received training in both areas through your previous roles, each school will have different personnel to alert and systems that they wish you to follow. It is likely that ICT forms part of the system, and you will need to know how to operate and populate any ICT-based system fairly rapidly for both behaviour management and safeguarding.

New ideas and new you

Flexibility and openness to new ideas are essential when you begin working in a new school. In England, schools and MAT have started to have authorial positions on educational and theoretical approaches to teaching. It is not unusual for a leader within a MAT or a school to issue an edict about how they expect staff to approach teaching pedagogically. You may find some of these edicts difficult or mystifying depending on your prior experience. For example, some schools and MATs seek to repress group work, seeing it as poor practice, which leads to cognitive overload and opportunities for pupils to disengage from their learning. Naturally, a strong teacher can teach a class using group work using well-evidenced approaches and good behaviour management. Indeed, some subjects such as drama and Physical Education (PE) have group work as central parts of their subjects. Being able to work within such systems is essential to your ability to teach and thrive in your new school. The reality is that the school seeks to eschew poorly undertaken group work and that is a fair aim – learning should always be of a high standard. In issuing edicts or trying to present a message in professional development programmes, schools or MATs can sometimes be clumsy in achieving this aim, and you may be left with the impression that the school or MAT does not really understand social constructivist teaching. Being able to operate within these tight lines is essential if you are to teach confidently in an evidence-informed way with high standards throughout your teaching.

Clear, precise and rapid communication

Schools and MATs thrive on communication. However, as teachers are usually teaching, much of this communication is electronic and as such is slow, asynchronous, time-consuming and often non-rapid. If the school or MAT is to deliver high-quality learning and interaction with parents, then rapid electronic communication is essential to the process. Many schools or MATs have adopted auto- and semi-automated systems for rapid communication. This can be as simple as enabling you to access on-call and support for behaviour incidents or to alert a parent that their child has not arrived for a lesson. Your role within this system is essential – not just to ensure that the school is working effectively in ensuring pupils are supported and teachers are working effectively in tandem, but also as part of safeguarding. Within the school, you will be expected to compose succinct communications ensuring that they are respectful and professional. For example, "CC-ing" senior or line managers into emails where you are keen for compliance to take place is seen as passive-aggressive bullying and creates workload for managers as well as a poor culture for colleagues. Other communication faux pas such as using emotional language or line-by-line quotations and response of another colleague's email really do not help a situation. Written communication, such as email or WhatsApp, is not a good medium for resolving conflicts. It is even worse when several people are involved, and you end up with a chain of messages which eventually gets taken to a senior leader to resolve. More effective is to set up a face-to-face meeting with your colleague and go to the meeting armed with solutions as well as problems. Be flexible and considerate, and you will find you earn yourself a reputation for fair and equitable leadership from the middle rather than a reputation for unhelpful communications.

Active participation in professional development

One area to consider is your conduct during professional development activities. Engaging in professional development opportunities allows teachers to develop their knowledge and skills, as well as being an opportunity to meet colleagues from across the school or MAT that they would not otherwise meet as part of being a member of a subject team. Attending workshops, conferences and training sessions both on and off-site can provide you with opportunities to develop your PLC and also demonstrate to others, especially managers and senior leaders, that you can be relied upon when it comes to developing and implementing interventions and strategies to enhance the learning experience of pupil in your school. Making an effort to learn people's names and roles, taking detailed notes, writing follow-up emails thanking someone for taking the time to deliver a session and also offering to liaise with further projects are all going to ensure that you are firmly embedded within a school and its joined-up approach to education. That is not to say you should be passive in your intake of ideas from professional development sessions. As a well-informed and read teacher, you should be ready to challenge misconceptions and ideas presented as fact rather than academic positions. An ongoing theme in this book is that teaching has changed. It is not that teachers have lost autonomy, but rather that the relationship between teachers and managers is now centred around evidential debates. For example, in a professional development session, a presenter might argue that working memory is limited and that a pupil can only hold between four and seven items in their memory. You might challenge this and say more recent research suggests we should look at "chunks" of working memory rather than isolated items and that others suggest working memory should be looked at in terms of "resolution." All three ideas have merit within a classroom where someone is trying to teach individual items of knowledge, collective chunks of knowledge where there are cued connections or where they might deliberately blur the resolution of a memory to teach something like the plot of a novel or an overarching view of a skeleton.

Demonstrating your strengths

This idea of bringing critically informed challenges to your work as a teacher is essential in helping you to forge a strong reputation as someone who is able to work in a critical environment without being tribal and whose ideas are helpful. As a teacher with a unique background of experiences and qualifications, you bring your strengths and talents to the teaching profession. The school community is strongest when it blends a range of teachers and professional services together and who all come from a rich tapestry of backgrounds. Whether you had a first career, grew up in another country, were educated in state, selective state, independent, single-sex schools or whatever, you bring with you your unique experiences. In addition, consider that your community is likely to have strengths and weaknesses. We know some people are absolute whizzes at technology, whereas others can defuse even the most tempestuous of children. We are very rarely great at all of these. Recognising your strengths and weaknesses and then ensuring your PLC knows this is your strength or weakness is important. Then your PLC knows when to support you or to call upon you for support. Even the slightest of things – like you have a unique interest that you are happy to share as an extra-curricular activity – really counts in a school. It is often the case that teachers operate outside of their natural subject areas for extra-curricular activities. For example, a Maths teacher could offer a cricket spin bowling session or an English teacher could offer a chess club. What is important is that the school community comes together to offer a rich and blended learning environment.

Liaising with colleagues is an essential part of the teaching profession, particularly in secondary schools where pupils interact with multiple teachers daily. Creating strong professional relationships with other teachers and middle or senior leaders is crucial for fostering a supportive and effective educational environment, as well as ensuring that you are a strong and autonomous teacher who plays an active role in delivering high-quality education.

Ultimately, liaising with colleagues is not just about maintaining professional relationships but about creating a community of practice where everyone works together, critically, to provide the best possible education for pupils. By fostering a culture of cooperation, criticality, respect and mutual support, teachers can contribute to a positive and productive school environment, benefiting both their colleagues and their pupils.

Enhancing the use of AfL in teaching

This section outlines practical strategies for embedding Assessment for Learning (AfL) into your teaching, whether you're working with General Certificate in Education (GCSE) or A-level pupils. At around three months into the academic year, you will likely have developed an understanding of your pupils' academic needs and their response to your teaching style. This familiarity makes it an ideal time to elevate your use of AfL to optimise pupil progress.

The importance of AfL in the classroom

AfL is a pedagogical approach that prioritises formative assessment, actively involving pupils in their own development. It provides timely feedback and supports adaptive teaching strategies. When applied effectively, AfL can transform the learning experience by identifying knowledge gaps, addressing misconceptions and fostering reflective learning.

This section explores methods such as whole-class feedback to reduce workload, the use of knowledge planners and organisers to evaluate learning and key opportunities for assessment, such as after a sequence of lessons or specific activities like essays or experiments. Resources from the Education Endowment Foundation (EEF) and the Chartered College of Teaching will also be examined.

AfL is not merely a set of tools but a critical method for evaluating the effectiveness of teaching and learning. It enables teachers to gather insights into pupils' understanding, adapt their instruction and foster deeper engagement. In exam-focused settings like GCSEs and A levels, where the curriculum is dense and stakes are high, AfL becomes particularly essential.

To use AfL effectively without creating unnecessary stress for teachers or pupils, consider the following principles:

Addressing Misconceptions: use AfL techniques to identify and address misconceptions during lessons. For example:

- **Art:** pupils might mistakenly start self-portraits with the face rather than the overall structure.
- **PE:** in cricket, pupils might believe batting is solely about power rather than technique and placement.

Embedding Formative Assessment: incorporate techniques such as questioning, mini whiteboards and peer assessment into every lesson to check understanding in real time.

Utilising Whole-Class Feedback: whole-class feedback allows you to address common errors without marking each piece of work individually. For instance, after marking a set of GCSE essays on the causes of World War II, you might highlight common issues such as weak use of evidence or poor structure. Using a feedback sheet and model answers, you can guide the class to improve their work collectively.

Providing Transparent Assessment Goals: pupils should always know how and what they will be assessed on, whether it is a short quiz, an essay or a summative test covering a unit. This transparency fosters a sense of ownership over their learning.

At this stage in the academic year, you should have sufficient understanding of your pupils to make informed decisions about adapting your teaching to meet their needs. While AfL focuses on formative assessment, summative assessments – such as at the end of a 4–6 lesson sequence or a half-term topic – also play a crucial role in evaluating progress and planning future teaching.

Strategies for effective AfL

Teachers in England use consistent approaches for effective AfL, and you would be expected to have learned these and be able to demonstrate them as part of meeting the teachers' standards. During department meetings, you will be expected to talk confidently about the different techniques, their effectiveness and also what they are telling you about your pupils. There will be standard practice for AfL in your school, but not all schools are the same. You should work on identifying some of the strategies being used and if any are not used. Some of the following strategies are typical of those that are often used.

Setting Clear Learning Objectives: begin each lesson with clear and measurable objectives that pupils can understand. When pupils know what they are expected to learn, they can focus their efforts more effectively. For example, a GCSE Geography lesson might include the objective: *"By the end of this lesson, you should be able to explain the causes of an earthquake and evaluate their impacts in different parts of the world."* Similarly, a GCSE History lesson could aim for pupils to *"explain the causes of World War II with links to World War I."* These objectives provide a roadmap for both teaching and assessment. However, being able to recall this learning in later lessons should also form part of future objectives. Remembering is an intrinsic part of learning for schools in England.

Using Diagnostic Assessment: at the start of a new topic or unit, use diagnostic tools to gauge pupils' prior knowledge. This might involve a quiz, a mind map or a discussion task. For example, in an A-level Biology class, a quiz on foundational concepts such as DNA structure and inheritance patterns can reveal knowledge gaps that guide your planning. This early insight helps tailor your teaching to address areas of weakness.

Embedding Formative Assessment Throughout Lessons: formative assessment should be a consistent element of every lesson. Techniques like questioning, peer assessment and the use of mini whiteboards allow you to monitor understanding and make adjustments as needed. For instance, in a GCSE Mathematics lesson, you might pose a hinge question such as: *"If the roots of the equation $x^2 + 5x + 6 = 0$ are -2 and -3, what are the roots of $x^2 + 5x - 6 = 0$?"* Pupils can respond on mini whiteboards, giving you immediate feedback on their comprehension.

Planning for Summative Assessment: summative assessments are equally important for measuring progress. These should be strategically placed, such as at the end of a sequence of lessons or a major activity. For example, in a GCSE English literature class, after studying *Romeo and Juliet*, an essay analysing themes of love and revenge could serve as a summative assessment. This approach consolidates learning while providing valuable data for future teaching.

Modern feedback methods: Reducing workload, maximising impact

Feedback is a cornerstone of AfL, but traditional marking practices can be time-consuming. Modern methods aim to provide impactful feedback while reducing workload, ensuring that pupils receive meaningful guidance on their progress. The ambition is to ensure your lessons are a feedback-rich environment rather than containing lots of ceremonial marking, which delivers minimal impact. The following methods will be common in many secondary schools, but you should ensure you are following expected practice within your department.

Whole-Class Feedback: instead of marking every piece of work in detail, whole-class feedback addresses common trends across pupils' submissions. For example, after reviewing Key Stage 3 essays on the US Civil Rights Movement, you might notice recurring issues such as weak argument structures or insufficient evidence. By preparing a feedback sheet highlighting these patterns, you can use the next lesson to address them with the whole class, incorporating model answers and targeted strategies for improvement.

Feedback Codes: feedback codes are a quick and effective way to highlight areas for improvement. These codes represent specific types of errors (e.g., SP for spelling, G for grammar, E for evidence) and can guide pupils in revising their work. For instance, in a GCSE Geography assignment, you might use *C* for content requiring more detail, *E* for missing case studies and *SP* for spelling corrections. Providing a key for these codes ensures pupils understand and act on the feedback.

Creating a Feedback-Rich Environment: a feedback-rich environment fosters ongoing dialogue between teachers and pupils. This can be achieved through regular formative assessments, peer review sessions and opportunities for self-assessment. Encouraging pupils to reflect on their progress and set goals for improvement creates a culture of continuous learning and growth.

By adopting these feedback methods, you can balance efficiency with effectiveness, ensuring that pupils receive the support they need while managing your workload.

Utilising AfL resources

Several organisations provide valuable resources and research on AfL strategies that can enhance your practice. Two key sources are the EEF and the Chartered College of Teaching.

Education Endowment Foundation (EEF)

The EEF provides evidence-based resources aimed at improving educational outcomes, particularly for disadvantaged pupils. Their toolkit on AfL offers practical advice on how to implement AfL strategies effectively.

The EEF's guidance report on effective feedback highlights strategies such as providing feedback that moves learning forward and ensuring that feedback is specific, actionable and related to learning objectives. Incorporating these strategies into your teaching can help create a more effective AfL environment.

Chartered College of Teaching

The Chartered College of Teaching offers professional development resources, including research articles, webinars and case studies on AfL. These resources can help you stay up-to-date with the latest developments in AfL and refine your practice.

You might use the Chartered College's resources to explore new approaches to AfL, such as using technology, to provide instant feedback or integrating peer assessment more effectively into your lessons.

AfL is not a one-size-fits-all

As you continue teaching your Key Stage 3, GCSE or A-level classes, stepping up your use of AfL can significantly enhance pupil learning and outcomes. By integrating AfL into your lesson planning, using modern feedback methods to reduce workload, employing knowledge organisers and strategically assessing knowledge, you can create a dynamic, feedback-rich environment that supports every pupil's progress.

Remember, however, that AfL is not a one-size-fits-all approach; it requires ongoing reflection and adaptation to meet the needs of your pupils. Utilise resources from the EEF and the Chartered College of Teaching to stay informed and inspired as you refine your AfL practice. With these strategies in place, you will be well-equipped to support your pupils in achieving their full potential.

Anxiety and stress

This section sets out that when changing schools, it is important to access support in the process of change. Teachers often move schools to create change in their working lives but that process of change leaves teachers having to cope with increased levels of anxiety and stress as a normal part of the process. Therefore, this chapter will explore some of the things that cause such stress such as senior leaders, scrutiny, parents and so forth and also recommend strategies for coping with such things. It will also set out what are unreasonable levels of stress and scrutiny and will also posit that sometimes it is necessary to look to move schools rapidly in order to leave such a system. By addressing common stressors and solutions, this chapter seeks to empower teachers with the tools and knowledge they need to navigate school changes successfully while maintaining their well-being.

Moving schools can induce stress

It is likely that one of the factors which has led you to read this book or chapter is that you have changed school environments. It might be that you have simply moved schools or MATs, you might have qualified recently as a teacher or you may have emigrated from another country to come and teach in England. Whichever the reason, moving to a new school can be an exciting prospect – fresh start, new colleagues and a refresh in systems and processes that you might have grown weary of. The reality is that you are in a state of transition and as such, this is a vulnerable time for you in which anxiety and stress are usual and typical things to experience as you adapt to the challenge of new systems, expectations and relationships.

New senior leaders

As much as senior leaders in schools and MATs try to prevent it, there is no escaping that their very presence brings stress and anxiety to some teachers, let alone their decisions, communications, policies and vision. Senior leaders collaborate to create a unique culture which reflects their attitudes and management styles. They have to convey expectations via specific communication styles, and the way they make decisions can vary from one school to another. Entering this new environment means adjusting and aligning to the new vision and new styles.

In some cases, you might rapidly find yourself struggling with the approach of the senior leadership, and this can lead to isolation or frustration. If you are used to a collaborative and supportive environment and have moved to a school that is more hierarchical and directive in design and style, then the immediate reaction will be that you find yourself undergoing stress. This book has tried to keep this as a theme running through the chapters – schools in England are less collaborative and autonomy has to, increasingly, be earned rather than given. You can do this by ensuring that the points you make are informed and backed up by wider reading and research. However, do be aware that in some schools or MATs, some senior leaders can be unsupportive and overly critical. They will be outliers, and it is right to note that the vast majority of senior leaders will be of a high quality. However, part of this book is about recognising when you are in an unhelpful position and that you need to rapidly move to another school. There are sections about when and how to resign or start looking for alternative employment. Even if you are a brand-new Early Career Teacher in your first year, if you find the leadership negative, overly critical and creating anxiety and other emotions in you, then do consider moving schools.

Scrutiny of your teaching standards "will" be different

Every school or MAT has its own system for ensuring that teaching standards are high. The nature of the system is only regulated once a senior leader decides a teacher needs support – first informal and then formal. As a teacher, you are protected by guidance from the Department of Education. This guidance is updated periodically, so you should make sure you are up-to-date with the latest guidance by googling "Teacher Capability – Guidance for schools when dealing with serious under-performance." In the guidance, it will set out what happens if you require informal support and what the process is for this to migrate to formal support. It is important that schools are able to hold teachers to account for their standards of teaching, but it is also important that teachers are treated fairly and for good reasons and not for reasons which they might see as excessive or unfair and which lead to anxiety and stress.

Integration is stressful

Whilst you may feel that your teaching standards are high at the start of your new school and that they are being recognised, there is no escaping you will also be feeling judged by your integration into the community of the school. Whether or not you feel accepted in the subject base room or in the wider staff room can create feelings of self-doubt and isolation. Sometimes, it might be that upon fraternising with others, you perceive some of their ideals are unrealistic and that you cannot and indeed will not step up to the levels of workload or expectations willingly. It is absolutely critical that you monitor for signs of burnout. Teachers frequently think they are leaving the profession, but in actual fact they are leaving a school and its leaders. One does not leave a school; one leaves a leader. If you do not think your new school is well-led, then be aware that other schools will be well-led and that you will feel supported and stretched in a healthy way at these other schools.

One aspect of moving to a new school that is stressful, which you might not realise, is the social side of moving school. You will likely not only have to build relationships with around 2–400 pupils but likely 50–100 fellow staff. You might struggle, at first, to find your place within the pre-existing staff dynamics. Indeed, your new presence will shift the staff dynamics, and we all know that change is hard for everyone. Existing staff will need to adapt to your new presence, and you will also have to forge new relationships across the school and MAT campuses. In a supportive and welcoming place, this is quick and easy to do. However, do not underestimate the strength of cliques or unspoken hierarchical structures. These informal power structures can be tricky, and it is easy to find this a challenge to navigate. This can be simple things such as where you put your resources or cup in a base or staff room to more complex things such as organising a trip which, unknown to know, competes with another member of staff. Informal consultation with safe, established and nurturing members of staff will help you navigate this. Do regular "kite flying" of ideas with these members of staff, and they will use their experience to let you know what the likely outcome will be. One last point to note is that some staff might come across as standoffish or unfriendly. Do not immediately judge these teachers. The reason is that teachers come from all walks of life, and some teachers, whilst being excellent in the classroom or on the playing field, may actually find social interaction challenging or even unnecessary! Not every teacher is warm and chatty, and you should not judge them for having dissimilar social interaction skills to yourself.

Parents and stress

You are teaching in loco parentis – in place of the parent, and so parents will have strong opinions about just how they like their child to be taught. They will sometimes have high expectations around communication between the teacher and the parents, as well as pupil outcomes. In changing schools, you will have changed typical parents and the parental culture that has evolved alongside the school. You should try to consult more established staff about the expectations of parents for the school, so that you can adapt readily and rapidly. It only takes one miscommunication for your name to feature in local WhatsApp and other social media groups. Be careful to ensure that all communications are via approved mediums, follow protocol and policy and are very formal in nature. Any miscommunications or misunderstandings with parents can lead to complaints or conflicts and as such can further exacerbate stressors for any new teacher to the school such as yourself. The alternate view is that long-standing relationships with parents who have more than one child moving through the school can be powerful and promote good outcomes for the pupils and reduce stress for yourself. Do not see your pupils as one-off pupils with you for just one or two years. See the pupils as part of a family, sometimes an extended family, with whom you and the school will have a long-standing relationship. That is the route to reducing stress and ensuring good outcomes across the board.

Curriculum and pedagogy

You will have learned specific ways of teaching your subject, and you will also have learned general pedagogical approaches to teaching. This combination of subject-specific and general pedagogical approaches is what makes you a teacher. However, schools in England have increasingly started to adopt established positions around pedagogical approaches, often driven by a single person in charge of teaching and learning who is reading around ideas and trying to implement them across a school or MAT through either professional development or through policies and processes. You may, upon beginning your new role, be handed a list of "non-negotiables." These are things that they expect every teacher to adhere to. This can be something like "Every lesson must start with 4 retrieval type questions" or "pupils must not put their hands up during questioning sessions." If you have come from a school where these sorts of rules were not implemented, you may find being in a school with rigid ideas about how to teach quite challenging and stressful. You might have evidence-informed objections to some of the approaches being prescribed to you and feel that it is an affront to your knowledge around teaching. However, this is part of the due diligence process you should be undertaking when moving schools. If such policies are that much of an affront to you, then the reality is that either you get on board with these things or the school is not for you.

It could be that the opposite is occurring. You may have come from a heavily regulated school environment where every class had a printed booklet, prescribed PowerPoint decks and detailed prescribed processes for the classroom from how to read with a ruler to what happens when the teacher speaks. If your new school is liberal and there are no booklets, but rather a folder of "recommended" PowerPoints, and freedom to adapt your pedagogy to your classes, then you might find such a change just as challenging and stressful as someone who is moving into your old environment. Change is difficult for all teachers, and the reality is that schools in England are increasingly diverse in how they expect teachers to go about their roles.

Strategies for managing stress

One key thing to remember when reflecting on whether you are feeling the stress as a teacher starting a new school is that you are not alone. And so, one of the most effective ways to manage stress during a school transition is to seek support from mentors and colleagues. Having people to go to, having a network of different types of colleagues from school receptionists to teachers in other subject departments, will help you access regular guidance, encouragement and perspective during the transition period and beyond. As a new teacher, whether experienced, new to the profession or from another country, you will be allocated a mentor of some kind who you can go to when you have questions that you do not want to take to your line manager. These mentors will be able to offer you valuable insights into the school or MAT's culture, expectations, policies and processes and at the same time help you, as a new teacher, navigate the challenges you face. Beyond your formal mentor, you should consider how you are integrating into the school. Consult the section in this book on integrating with colleagues. This is important because cultivating and sharing a sense of camaraderie and mutual support can help alleviate any feelings of isolation and stress you might experience at the start of your new role.

One of the main causes of stress and anxiety for you will be your own expectations and boundaries that you set for yourself. Too often, teachers looking to make a splash at a new school start with tremendous ambitions. They will agree to staff numerous events, pledge to organise further events and then try to give themselves unrelenting expectations around their actual teaching. The reality rapidly hits home when they hit the first pinch point of the year. For example, you might get six sets of ends of topics tests to mark with a parent evening due within two weeks of receiving the test sets. In addition, you have regular teaching and marking to do whilst covering all of the extra-curricular activities you had pledged to do. The only space this time can come from is your personal life, and then if anything crops up there, you can end up in a position where you see no option but to get signed off by the doctor with stress. Your school and your line manager do not want to see you signed off with stress. They want to see you organised and managing your day-to-day teaching first before you step up to undertake further activities. An experienced teacher who has taught the materials several times over and who has got the rise and fall of the school year just right will be able to juggle these things early on and it is important to see that the reason they can do this is because of their experience and the length of time they have been working in the school.

Setting realistic boundaries is critical for your ability to manage your stress levels. This means being able to say no when asked to take on additional responsibilities that are not essential. It also means having clear boundaries around levels of communication with pupils and parents through the official technological systems that are used within your school to enable you to communicate with pupils and parents safely. You might be tempted to sacrifice some self-care and well-being in your efforts to make a good impression in your new school. However, this is a fallacy because energy borrowed will eventually need to be paid back, and you will find yourself working in a state of exhaustion. You should continue to pursue activities and hobbies that you find relaxing and healthy and which promote your well-being. Things like exercise or sports, especially with non-teachers where you are unable to talk about teaching or work. In addition, you should consider how much time you are making available for family and friends. You are looking to establish long-term patterns and maintaining family and friendships are part of that.

One other approach to managing stress will be your resilience to stress itself. Change is a normal thing, and, indeed, there is such a thing as healthy levels of stress. A lack of stress can sometimes be the reason we change schools or train to become a teacher. We identify the challenges of teaching or being in a new school as something that is desirable to achieve or experience. Thinking about this philosophically when you realise you are experiencing the symptoms of stress is a critical part of managing it. At a healthy level, stress is exciting and thrilling and drives us to achieve tremendous things, and even after the event, we remain enthused and fulfilled by the experience. Setbacks, unexpected challenges, receiving unexpected feedback and so forth are all part of a healthy level of stress as part of taking on a new challenge – as well as being part of an unhealthy level of stress. How, then, do we distinguish the difference between the two? This is especially true if you have come from a difficult school who have used excessive scrutiny and challenge as a way of moving you on from your school.

The answer lies in the narrative that emerges from middle and senior leaders. Strong leaders want their staff, and especially new staff, to respond well to challenges. They know this means they will need to put in place good on-boarding systems, buddies, mentors and be open to requests for help. Weak leaders will bully staff and try to make them face up to challenges through fear and intimidation. If this is the leadership which you find yourself experiencing, then we recommend you review the sections of this book titled: last day for resignations to start work in… This will help you to plan a move to a new school where strong leadership exists.

An important point to consider is that every teacher is a leader, and this includes you, even if you are an Early Career Teacher or brand new to the school. That means showing leadership within your communications to senior and middle leaders, parents and other professionals within your school community. You should be assertive in your communication, especially when setting boundaries or addressing what you perceive as unreasonable demands. You should feel empowered to advocate for your own needs and well-being rather than immediately resort to union involvement. You will find that middle and senior leaders respect someone happy to talk face to face, calmly and reasonably about their misgivings or concerns, and this can often lead to better relationships going forward. Difficult conversations are part of being a teacher, and this means not shying away from them and approaching them with confidence and professionalism.

Unreasonable stress

Whilst we are keen to embrace reasonable stress and challenge as part and parcel of the fulfilling job of being a secondary teacher, there is still a line where it turns into unreasonable stress and scrutiny and it is important to be able to recognise the point at which it becomes either unreasonable or, alternatively, unhealthy. The first things to look for are physical symptoms such as chronic fatigue, headaches or sleep disturbances, as well as emotional symptoms such as anxiety, irritability or depression. This tends to come along with a decreasing standard in your performance and motivation.

One particular manifestation of unreasonable stress is through excess scrutiny and accountability – particularly if it is punitive or disproportionate. It is well documented in legions of lived experiences from teachers that they moved on from a school after being unfairly targeted or their work was micromanaged to an unreasonable degree. Relentless scrutiny, especially if accompanied by a lack of support or sensible and constructive feedback, tells you that your school environment is toxic and causing you unreasonable stress.

It is not always senior leaders who are the cause of such excessive stress. Sometimes, middle leaders can be guilty of poor leadership and are unable to lead their departments or work towards an external metric such as examination outcomes in a way that is supportive and fair. If your school or department environment is characterised by excessive pressure, lack of support or a toxic culture, it may be necessary to act. You should consider whether the stress and scrutiny you are experiencing are likely to improve over time or whether they are indicative of deeper systemic issues within the school. If you find yourself in an untenable situation, it may be necessary to seek external support and professional advice. This could involve consulting with a union representative, seeking legal advice through an organisation such as EDAPT (a subscription-based, non-union source of legal advice) or accessing support services available through your MAT, such as counselling. It is also important to remember that you are not alone in facing these challenges. Connecting with professional networks or support groups of teachers can provide a sense of solidarity and shared experience, as well as practical advice and support. If you make the decision to leave, it is important to do so thoughtfully and strategically. This will involve securing a new position before resigning (if possible), carefully considering the timing of the departure and leaving on good terms with colleagues and leadership in order to secure a good reference. By taking these steps, you can ensure a smoother transition to a more positive and supportive environment.

Changing schools means an increase in necessary stress

Changing schools can be a significant and often challenging step in any teacher's career. While moving to a new school can bring about stress and anxiety, it also offers opportunities for growth, learning and professional development. By understanding the common stressors associated with moving to a new school and implementing strategies to manage them, you can navigate this temporary period of acclimatisation with confidence and resilience.

Last day for resignations to start work in January

This section provides essential guidance for teachers in England on applying for jobs, understanding resignation deadlines and navigating employment-related decisions. It aligns with the principles outlined in the Burgundy Book, ensuring compliance with standard practices. You can read this guidance by googling the term "burgundy book." The burgundy book is a handbook setting out the conditions of service for schoolteachers in England and Wales. Its main provisions relate to notice periods, sick leave and pay and maternity leave and pay. Teachers must give two months' notice at all times, except for the final term, in which the notice is three months.

During your time at your current school, whether you have been there for four weeks or four years, it is important to note the end-of-October resignation deadline if you wish to leave at the end of the December term to start at a new school in January. Before submitting your resignation to the school's HR team and discussing your plans with the headteacher, consider the following steps:

Seek sound advice

Consult your head of department or trusted colleagues about your decision. While others may have experienced similar challenges, they might choose to remain in their roles. Be aware that their advice could reflect their own coping mechanisms and might not fully align with your circumstances. Use their perspectives to inform, but not dictate, your decision-making process.

Plan your exit with diplomacy

If you decide to leave by December and start the new year in a different role, it is crucial to approach your departure with strategic diplomacy. Remember, you will need a reference from your current employer. While references must, by law, be factual and fair, they may lack enthusiasm if your exit is perceived negatively. To maintain professional relationships, communicate your reasons for leaving tactfully and focus on your aspirations for growth rather than dwelling on negative experiences.

Prepare early

To meet the October resignation deadline, you must have begun job searching and scheduling interviews well in advance. For those who started their current roles in September, this might mean initiating a job hunt within weeks of joining. Transparency with your line manager and HR is vital if you need to request time off for interviews so soon after starting. Honest communication can help you secure their understanding and support.

By carefully considering these factors and adhering to the resignation deadlines outlined in the Burgundy Book, you can navigate your transition smoothly and set yourself up for a positive start in your next role.

November 20 days

Introduction

November is a busy month with a dual focus on supporting pupils with their university applications and preparing for mock examinations. This chapter provides guidance on the UCAS process, including Oxbridge applications, interview preparation and writing personal statements. It also covers how to set up and effectively prepare pupils for mock exams, utilising exam board reports, past papers and departmental moderation to ensure high-quality preparation.

UCAS applications

This section provides guidance on supporting pupils with their university applications in the UK. It covers the UCAS process for both Oxbridge and other universities, preparing pupils for interviews (especially for Oxbridge or PSRB courses requiring mandatory interviews), and supporting colleagues in writing personal statements. Teachers who work with Key Stage 5 pupils will often contribute to the application process by providing predicted grades or recommendations. Understanding the new 2024 UCAS process can also help teachers advise younger pupils, especially those from non-traditional higher education backgrounds, promoting greater equity of knowledge and embedding cultural capital.

Preparing pupils for university applications

Aspiration for a university education can be one possible destination of a pupil's school journey. However, encouraging pupils to aspire towards higher education may involve addressing barriers such as social and economic backgrounds, cultural expectations and concerns about higher education debt. You can play a key role by:

- Organising visits to universities for Year 9 pupils to inspire long-term thinking. Many universities offer open days or summer schools that your pupils can take advantage of.

- Collaborating with university outreach departments to ensure pupils receive adequate exposure to higher education opportunities.

- Highlighting the broader value of a university education beyond financial returns, including personal development, independence and networking opportunities.

Cultivating passion and knowledge for university degrees

Helping pupils connect their interests to potential degree choices is crucial. Within Key Stage 5 teaching, informal discussions about career pathways can make a significant impact. For example:

- Physics teachers might discuss chemical engineering degrees.

- Health and Social Care teachers could introduce degrees in hospitality.

- Teachers of Art, Graphics and Computer Science might explore emerging fields like animation, design, coding and fintech.

Stay informed about both traditional and new degree options. Spend time reviewing the UCAS website or university prospectuses to understand entry requirements and course structures. Advise pupils on the types of questions to ask at UCAS fairs or open days, such as:

- Graduate outcomes and employment links.

- Student-to-lecturer ratios and quality of teaching scores.

- Dropout rates and accommodation options.

- Campus facilities and industry connections.

Supporting Oxbridge applicants

Applications to Oxford and Cambridge are due in October, earlier than the January deadline for other universities. They also usually require specific GCSEs and A levels for their courses and it is essential your pupils and their parents know this from when the pupil is a young age. This application process requires significant preparation during Year 12 because they will not have time to do this if they wait until Year 13 like they might for non-Oxbridge applications. Pupils should:

- Visit a range of colleges to understand the differences, such as location, facilities and alumni networks. For example, Churchill College at Cambridge may be far from the English faculty, while Jesus College at Oxford is known for its sports facilities.

- Decide whether to apply to a specific college or submit an open application, which allows central administration to allocate them a college.

You should encourage spring and summer visits to colleges to help pupils make informed choices. Outreach departments from Oxbridge will be pleased to support you and your pupils with this. Simply Google Cambridge or Oxford "outreach" and the first websites will contain helpful links and contact information.

Early applications for medicine and dentistry

Medicine and dentistry courses also have early application deadlines. Encourage pupils in Year 12 to:

- Visit universities to explore reputation, accommodation, course structure and proximity to home.
- Gain relevant work experience during the summer, such as volunteering in a pharmacy, local GP surgery or healthcare setting.

PSRB and Oxbridge courses require interviews!

For courses governed by Professional, Statutory and Regulatory Bodies (PSRBs), such as Medicine, Teaching, Nursing, Law and Engineering, interviews assess both academic potential and professional aptitude. Unlike Oxbridge interviews, which focus on academic discussion, PSRB interviews often include scenario-based questions, ethical dilemmas and communication skills assessments. For example, applications to teaching may ask you questions about safeguarding to ensure that you would keep children safe during specific scenarios during a school placement.

Coaching pupils for interviews

Teachers can make a real difference in preparing pupils for interviews, especially those from underrepresented backgrounds or first-generation university applicants. For Oxbridge interviews, pupils should:

- Practice thinking aloud, explaining their reasoning during mock interviews.
- Engage with academic material beyond the curriculum to build confidence.
- Learn techniques to stay calm under pressure.

Mock interviews and feedback

Mock interviews help pupils prepare, with detailed feedback on content, critical thinking, communication and body language. Where possible, involve external professionals for fresh perspectives. You should consider working with your school to help organise evenings designed to provide interview practice for your pupils who will have to undertake an entrance interview as part of their application to university.

Supporting personal statements

Personal statements are vital for UCAS applications. Teachers should guide pupils in structuring their statements, focusing on academic achievements, relevant work experience and extracurricular activities, while offering constructive feedback without overstepping and writing them for them. Encourage early drafts and provide feedback that balances praise and constructive criticism.

Contributing to UCAS references and predicted grades

Predicted grades, based on data like mock exams and sometimes coursework, are key in the UCAS process. Be realistic but supportive, explaining predictions to pupils to manage expectations. UCAS references should highlight academic performance, personal qualities and potential for success.

Navigating UCAS changes

Stay informed about UCAS changes, such as the shift towards digital literacy, more flexible offers and enhanced support for disadvantaged pupils. These changes offer new opportunities, and teachers should help pupils navigate them effectively. There might be access opportunities for your pupils. Google "Oxbridge Access Programme" to see what support is currently available.

Be their guide

Your role as a teacher is pivotal in guiding pupils through the university application process, from interview preparation to supporting personal statements and references. By staying informed and fostering equity, you can help create a more informed and accessible pathway to higher education for all your pupils.

Preparing for mock examinations

This section outlines how to set up mock examinations for Key Stages 4 and 5 and effectively prepare pupils for them. The focus is on utilising exam board reports from previous summer exams, past papers and departmental moderation to ensure high-quality preparation. These mock exams are typically held before the end of term and may be the first in a series that will continue before the official exam period in May. Many schools now operate double mock examinations, and you should check your school calendar or head of department to know exactly what and when your pupils will be given a mock examination. In addition, the mock examinations cause workload and you will need to be very organised to ensure your papers are marked in time.

Know your pupils

To effectively track pupils' progress, you should maintain detailed records of what they know, what they understand well and the areas where they need support. This can be done using school-approved software for tracking and reflecting on learning. These records should not just show simple numbers, like whether a pupil is on Grade 7 or two grades below expectations. Instead, use the opportunity to highlight gaps in core knowledge or skills required for success in the subject and its exams if it has any (all pupils will undertake at KS4, but not all will sit GCSE examinations in the subject). This information will help you target areas for development and guide your intervention strategies. Keep in mind, however, that there are many elements of the curriculum that pupils will need to know, and assessment for learning (AFL) can help guide your focus. Do not be overly critical of yourself if there are gaps – it is a natural part of the learning process. This can be especially daunting if you pick up a Year 11 or a Year 13 class in a new school and find their knowledge or skills are patchy due to exposure to temporary teaching provision.

Replicate conditions

The conditions of the summer exams cannot be fully replicated in the mock exams, especially when taken in the cold, damp exam hall of a December morning. The pressure of the "last chance" for success will not be there either. However, you can assist the school to create a realistic experience for pupils by focusing on the logistics of the exam. This includes making sure they are familiar with the expectations, using clear pencil cases, and bringing water bottles with no labels. They should also know how to remain silent for 1–3 hours and memorise their candidate ID numbers and the centre number. These procedures should be practised during the mocks to help them prepare for the real exams in May–June.

Collaborate and moderate

To ensure all pupils are assessed fairly, collaborate with your colleagues regularly to align on which topics have been covered, especially if you are teaching Year 9 to Year 11. If a topic has not been covered consistently across the department, the exam paper may need to be adjusted. This collaboration ensures that all pupils are answering the same types of questions.

Looking at past exam papers from the previous 3–5 years is a great way to identify patterns in question style and content. Pay attention to the types of questions the exam board tends to ask, and the kinds of texts or examples used in the exams, whether for History, R.E., English or other subjects. Be careful not to use the same questions from practice papers in your lessons, as pupils will recognise them, and their responses will skew the data. Using familiar questions may give a false sense of preparation and will lead to inaccurate assessments of their abilities.

In addition to reviewing past papers, make sure to examine the exam board's reports on previous years. These reports provide a breakdown of the overall cohort's performance, offering insights into how different groups of pupils handled specific types of questions. This may have already been done by your head of department, but it is vital that you, as the class teacher, are aware of the feedback. For example, if a 12-mark question on Geography was answered poorly due to a lack of depth in the case study response, you can adjust your teaching to focus on this weakness. Similarly, if a 4-mark question on stem cells showed that many pupils mislabelled diagrams, you can address these common mistakes before the next assessment.

When it comes to marking and moderating exam papers, there are three key practices you should follow. First, it is essential to moderate your marking with other teachers to determine what you believe constitutes a definite Grade 3 or Grade 7. Your head of department will likely arrange this, but you will need to undertake some standardisation work before the moderation meeting. Interpretation of grade boundaries can vary, so it is important to engage in discussions with your department to ensure consistency. Knowing what each grade boundary looks like will help you participate effectively in this process.

Mock exams lead to better teaching

Lastly, use the mock exam results to inform your teaching for the months leading up to the final exams. Mocks are a valuable tool for identifying areas where pupils need more support, and this insight should guide your planning from January to April. Adjust your teaching strategies based on what the mocks reveal about pupils' strengths and weaknesses. The data you collect will allow you to target intervention efforts more effectively, ensuring that all pupils are prepared for the real exams.

Form tutor parent evenings

This section sets out how to prepare for pastoral parent evenings or days, ensuring that parents leave feeling satisfied and pupils are better supported in their work. It covers preparation for meetings that focus on pastoral issues, academic progress reports and fostering positive relationships with parents or carers. It also discusses how to use data from the pastoral and year teams to support these relationships. Additionally, it explores how to adapt your register, tone and phrases depending on the nature of the conversations.

The form tutor is the bridge

As you build your relationship with your form group, you will begin to realise that you are a vital figure in their development as young people. The pupils may not always understand it, but you do. You offer them guidance on moral development, character building, resolving conflicts with friends and others in school and helping them make sense of the world we all share. To be an effective tutor, there are several strategies and actions that you need to employ.

Firstly, you are the bridge that links and supports your tutees with the rest of the school. You will need to relay information, gather insights and report back to colleagues, and your mode of communication must be clear and effective. For example, if the pastoral team needs to know who witnessed an incident in the dining room, you must be able to obtain this information and pass it on. Similarly, if you need to know which pupils may not have access to an electronic device for a technology-based activity, such as completing a survey or homework, you need to communicate this to other colleagues who may set tasks that rely on having these resources at home. It is also important to keep the library and pupil support services informed about the number of pupils who require access to resources.

There will be a pastoral curriculum that complements the academic curriculum. This curriculum is part of the wider learning that pupils need, covering topics such as recycling, bullying, healthy eating, sports competitions, quizzes, World Book Day, current affairs, fundraising and personal hygiene and safety. These activities are designed to help pupils become well-rounded individuals, ready for life beyond the classroom. As a tutor, your level of engagement, inspiration, and understanding will have a significant impact on your learning. If you are personally engaged in reducing your carbon footprint and actively promoting recycling, your enthusiasm will make these topics more authentic and inspiring for your pupils. This is a fantastic opportunity for you to really get to know your tutees, as some may have interests beyond the school curriculum. These moments allow pupils to showcase their passions and engage in meaningful discussions.

As a form tutor, you must be able to absorb and act on a wide range of issues affecting your tutees. It is essential to understand the systems within the school and be clear about your responsibilities, as well as those of others. For example, if a pupil keeps getting sent out of an English lesson, is it your role to investigate the issue, or is it the responsibility of the head of English? If it is not your responsibility, what should you do to support the pupil? Similarly, if there is a fight between tutees in your form, how do you ensure that other members of staff, who may teach them in other subjects, are informed? Is it your responsibility to communicate this, or is it the role of the senior leader handling the issue? Each school will have its own systems and procedures, you must be sure to follow the systems in your new school, not your old school.

Your role as a form tutor is to act as a bridge of support, communication and information between your tutees and their parents or carers. Before the parent evening, reflect on if some parents or carers are able to attend. Some may not be able to attend, so you should make alternative provisions in line with the school's policy. The process begins with initial communication, then the evening itself, and any necessary follow-up. You should not view the evening as an isolated event; it is part of an ongoing, fluid relationship.

The parent evening may take place either online or in person, and it will require you to transmit and explain various data points. When discussing attendance, academic progress or behaviour, there are a few key points to keep in mind. You must clearly set out the purpose of the meeting. It is not an informal chat; the aim is to address concerns, offer praise for notable achievements, and follow the required procedures. It may be the only opportunity you have to speak with parents in detail, so make the most of it.

Do not make assumptions about parents based on their appearance. Just because a parent is dressed well or works in a professional field, it does not necessarily mean they will understand the data you present. Conversely, do not assume that a parent who is less formally dressed will not understand the information you present. It is important to have a consistent approach that ensures you do not inadvertently offend anyone.

You will have a limited time slot, and parents may ask questions that require more detailed answers or additional support from other colleagues, such as subject heads or the pastoral team. Be prepared to send follow-up emails or arrange phone calls to address these queries.

Parent evenings should not be viewed as one-off events but as part of an ongoing relationship with parents and carers. Use these opportunities to build trust, celebrate pupils' achievements and collaboratively address any challenges they face, ensuring that they receive the best support possible.

End of unit assessments

This section sets out how to approach end-of-unit assessments and ensure the data is usable if the school does any form of data drops. It will cover how to ensure high-quality of "planning for assessments" leads to enough relevant content being covered in lessons and that revision and recall opportunities have been built into homework or lesson time. It will go into detail about the logistics needed such as location of the assessment, resources required such as specialist equipment and that SEND needs have been met through liaison with the SEND coordinator (SENDCO). Details about planning will be offered such as ensuring that they do not clash with out-of-lesson trips, assemblies or even after P.E lessons where pupils may be late due to changing. It will develop a work-life balance by setting out how to make sure that you have planned enough time to mark the assessment and offer opportunities for absent pupils to take it in an appropriate setting.

Tracking data

For many years, secondary school teachers in England were required to complete "data drops", entering half-termly test results into school-wide spreadsheets that monitored pupil progress using flight paths – an outdated method of tracking progress. These tests, however, often measured very different skills. A test on grammar, for instance, is fundamentally different from one analysing Shakespeare, just as a pupil might excel in performing a dramatic piece but struggle with writing an essay in drama. Across subjects, whether comparing creative writing to poetry analysis or fine art drawing to essays on art history, it becomes clear that such data points are not comparable and cannot serve as a reliable "flight path" of progress.

This created problems for teachers, who often found themselves on improvement plans based on pupils' fluctuating scores – fluctuations that were more reflective of the type of topic assessed than any decline in teaching quality. Despite this, teachers still need meaningful ways to assess whether pupils have learned the curriculum and developed the necessary skills. End-of-topic or unit tests remain essential, but the focus should be on ensuring that these assessments are meaningful and informative, rather than forcing comparisons that don't align with the content or skills being measured.

Planned and integrated assessment

If you teach a range of knowledge and skills throughout a topic and then, for the very first time, at the end of the topic, introduce a test that the pupils have never seen before, then don't expect good outcomes. As a working rule of thumb, you want to spend one-third of your teaching time on preparing for an end-of-topic assessment and two-thirds of your teaching time on teaching new knowledge and skills. You are not just teaching your pupils the knowledge and skills they need to know and perform, but you are teaching them how to express that knowledge and skills in assessment situations. One only has to read the annual examiner reports for each secondary school subject to see all the mistakes that teachers of specific subjects are making around their teaching of assessment strategies. End-of-topic or end-of-unit tests are an opportunity for you to develop your ability to do well in assessment situations, not just to learn the topic. You should be familiar with the examiner reports for your subject and their annual recommendations – this is an expected standard of teaching knowledge in secondary schools in England.

Rather than spending lots of time on whole test practice, you want to adopt micro assessments, which enable pupils to explore and learn tiny parts of an assessment. If you are teaching a key stage four class, then the assessment could be as small as a one-mark question or, if your subject is arts or humanities, it could be how to write an opening paragraph for an extended essay worth up to 20 marks. What this tells you is that foundation of a successful end-of-topic or unit assessment lies in its design. High-quality planning, by you, should ensure that the assessment aligns with the key objectives and content of the unit. This means that in the lessons leading up to the assessment you must not only comprehensively cover the necessary material, but consider how revisiting, recall and revision are built in alongside understanding the method and inner workings of the assessments they will undertake. Standard AFL practice in secondary schools in England means that you should be repeating a sequence of teaching knowledge or skills (along with memory-related strategies to ensure strong memories and recall are present) along with the micro-assessment that will be checking whether a pupil can demonstrate the knowledge or skill at a later point in time.

One aspect of end-of-topic or unit tests to consider is how you will address the needs of pupils with special educational needs and disabilities (SEND). You should liaise with the school's SENDCO and any teaching assistants well in advance to allow for any necessary accommodations to be made, whether that involves providing additional time, ensuring accessible materials, or arranging for alternative formats. You should also speak to the pupils involved so that they understand you want the assessment to *accurately* measure their knowledge and skills and to understand that you want to learn from them about what they find difficult in any assessment you deliver that is over and above the difficult or challenge for any other pupil. In addition, try to involve parents in any end-of-topic tests as they often are closely involved with their children and will want to support their child to ensure they achieve the maximum outcomes they can in your assessments. This collaboration from you with others will help to create an equitable assessment environment, where all pupils have the opportunity to demonstrate their knowledge and skills.

Timing of assessments

A large feature of importance in secondary schools is the timing of end-of-topic assessments. Consider if last lesson on a Friday is really the best time to assess the knowledge of your pupils or if there is a more suitable slot. Even very basic considerations such as being aware if a lesson is happening immediately before the test or checking the school calendar to see if there are trips, assemblies or other events which could clash with or disrupt the assessment schedule. By being strategic and considerate you can ensure that the assessment is not only smooth and fair but is accurately measuring what a pupil can do or know.

In addition to timing for pupils, think about timings for yourself. Marking assessments takes considerable time and you need to schedule the marking and return of the marks to ensure a well-organised process. Ensure you tell pupils exactly when they will be getting their outcomes returned, as they will question you for this information at every opportunity if you do not!

Lastly, have in place a contingency plan for those who might miss the assessment for illness or other reasons. How can you ensure that the rescheduled test does not lead to missing further education or, indeed, stress and worry? Tell pupils in advance what the consequences are if they miss a test so that they know if they are absent for whatever reason they will have another opportunity to take the assessment.

It is by being strategic, considerate and open about assessments that you will maximise the positive outcomes of the assessments and ensure you learn, accurately, how well your pupils have learned the content of your curriculum.

December 15 days

Introduction

As the year winds down, December emphasises the importance of planning using data and adaptive teaching. This chapter explains how to use assessment data to inform and adapt your teaching strategies. It covers identifying patterns of success and failure, addressing common mistakes and implementing evidence-informed practice. The goal is to ensure that teaching is responsive to the needs of all pupils, helping them achieve their best outcomes.

Planning using data

This section explains how schools increasingly expect teachers to use data to inform and adapt their teaching. Once you have assessed your classes, there will be a mark book or a data system where this information is collated. From this data, you will be able to identify patterns of success and failure, common mistakes in learning and opportunities to improve your teaching by planning accordingly. Additionally, it will cover the concept of evidence-informed practice, helping you understand how your wider reading can influence interventions and adaptations to centralised planning.

Data drops

Although data drops are still common in many school settings and often used to show progress, this can sometimes be misleading. Once the data has been interpreted, action, often in the form of intervention, may be required. This could be targeted at specific pupils, or it could focus on a particular topic or unit that may have been misunderstood.

Rationale for data

Data usage differs from school to school, though in a multi-academy trust (MAT), it is often applied in similar ways across the schools involved. Data can be presented in many forms, and how it is understood by teachers and pupils varies. As a priority, you must request training on the specific data analysis methods used by your school. This is because the methods will be focused on the metrics by which you and your colleagues are measured and those which senior leaders value. Being knowledgeable about important metrics is vital to ensure your start at your new school is successful. Remember, data are used to measure pupils' progress and development and to identify patterns that could lead to interventions. It will also be used in both internal and external evaluations of your school, so it is essential that you understand it thoroughly.

Identifying patterns

After conducting an assessment, you may notice patterns emerging. For example, in a Mathematics end-of-unit test, you might find that many pupils struggled to show their workings or that a specific question on algebra was answered poorly. By reviewing your lesson on algebra, you can try to identify why many pupils struggled with this topic. In a Geography GCSE test, you might find that certain questions on Natural Hazards were answered well, but the language used was not geographical – it was too general. This would suggest the need for more focus on using key geographical terms. Additionally, you might notice that English as an Additional Language (EAL) pupils performed very well, but a significant number of boys were underachieving. By reflecting on the behaviour of these boys and reviewing behaviour data, you may discover a pattern of underachievement linked to pupils who were often late for class or had higher rates of absence. These insights can guide your next steps in both teaching and interventions.

Measuring progress

The journey that pupils are on may not always be fully understood by them, but as teachers, you will see their progress, and data will provide evidence to support this. For example, in Physical Education (PE), a pupil who has begun to grasp the rules of rugby and no longer throws the ball forwards after four lessons, but is now developing ball-handling skills, shows progress. In basketball, as they improve further with skills such as dribbling and communicating more effectively with teammates, their progress is clear. You might then focus on different sets of skills in the same subject, such as bat and ball control in hockey, or in racket-based individual sports like tennis or badminton. Again, progress should be documented, and data from observations can then be used to track improvement.

In written-based subjects such as English, History and Geography, progress can be measured by how pupils are able to use evidence to support their arguments and develop their writing skills to sustain a narrative. If pupils struggle with this, intervention will need to be used to support their progress. Data from assessments will highlight areas of need, and specific actions can be planned to help pupils improve in these areas – and the school senior leaders will expect you to be able to demonstrate that this is happening.

Drawing conclusions from data

The data you collect should be used to draw conclusions about your pupils' progress and identify areas where intervention may be needed. In some schools, data is used to evaluate a teacher's effectiveness, but it can also be used to explain why some pupils are not making the expected levels of progress. When this happens, intervention strategies will be necessary. These might include after-school revision sessions or adapting your classroom teaching to better meet the needs of pupils who lack certain competencies.

For example, in a Geography GCSE class, you may have a pupil who writes well, using appropriate subject-specific terminology and is clearly explaining their answers. However, they might be limited in their use of case studies – which are critical for higher-level responses. To address this, an intervention could focus on helping the pupil develop stronger links to case studies. This might involve a simple mnemonic, such as "C" for "case study", to help the pupil remember to include case studies in their responses.

Similarly, in a History GCSE class, pupils may struggle with making judgments in their essays, which is essential for achieving higher grades. You could use targeted intervention to help pupils understand how to make clear, evidence-based judgments in their written work. This could involve providing examples of strong, judgement-based responses and giving pupils the tools to practise and apply this skill in their own writing.

Interventions and actions

Once you have analysed the data and identified areas for improvement, interventions can be targeted at individual pupils or entire cohorts, depending on the patterns you observe. For example, if a significant number of pupils in your class are struggling with the same topic or concept, whole-class interventions or revisiting the topic in a different way might be appropriate.

In some cases, interventions will be specific to certain skills. For example, if you identify that a pupil has mastered the basics of a subject but struggles with more complex tasks, you may need to provide additional support in that area. This could involve adaptive tasks, small-group work, or one-to-one support, depending on the needs of the pupil.

By using data to inform your teaching and interventions, you are ensuring that every pupil has the opportunity to make progress. The data provides you with valuable insights into how your pupils are performing, what needs to be revisited and where targeted support can make a difference. Through evidence-informed practice, you can ensure that interventions are based on sound research and strategies that have been shown to be effective in supporting pupil learning.

Adaptive teaching

This section sets out how teachers will begin to adapt their teaching for each child as they learn more about their specific learning needs. It will articulate how helping each pupil attain strong outcomes is a vital part of having an egalitarian education system. It will cover a specific part of teaching in England – the transition from differentiated learning to adaptive learning and it will set out the rationale for no longer giving different resources, activities or tasks to specific pupils. In this vein, it will cover strategies for helping SEND pupils achieve high outcomes both within lessons and through pre-lesson adaptations.

Diversity of learners varies from school to school

Secondary schools in England contain a diverse range of learners across a range of demographics and learning needs. As such, the children you will meet in your school are likely to be wholly different from children that you taught in another school. These differences have shaped their journey through education and will have resulted in, hopefully, responsive teaching strategies that target the varying needs of each pupil. In England, there is a strong vision of an egalitarian educational system in which every pupil competes in a meritocracy for examination grades and learning experiences. The reality is that the English secondary school educational system struggles to reduce in-built social disadvantages. This results in lower outcomes for those from deprived backgrounds, and even more so for those who do not live in London and the Southeast of England, and those with special educational needs and/or disabilities (SEND). How, then, to approach secondary education if such disadvantages are entrenched?

Some of the answer comes from understanding statistics. Whilst it is true that, overall, outcomes are lower for some pupils than others, it also remains true that some pupils from SEND or deprived backgrounds and also some schools with large numbers of pupils from SEND or deprived backgrounds do better than their national statistical outcomes. You should start with a premise of high expectations. It matters not that your pupil has EAL or that they have impaired sight or any other learning need – your mindset must be on believing that this pupil is capable of achieving great things. Indeed, it may be that a pupil will achieve great things regardless of the quality of teacher they experience. A pupil that is self-regulated to a high degree can turbo-charge their learning regardless of the school or teacher which they experience. If we couple such a child with a high-quality teacher and school, then we can see how such pupils can make progress that belies the national statistics for their particular demographic or learning need.

Historically, the way to adapt for a child with specific needs was to differentiate for them. This meant offering different work of different difficulties. Teachers would plan lessons which offered different levels of work for their pupils to access. Sometimes, they would hide this by dressing it up with language such as

"Gold, Silver or Bronze" or "Grande, Venti, Trenta". Whichever system was used, the outcome was the same, pupils were either allocated a level or were encouraged to select the level they felt was most appropriate to them. It got to the point where teachers were printing several sets of resources for every lesson with different coloured paper for all the subgroups and suffering with workload burnout trying to cater for these pupils using this method. This approach has now changed in English Secondary Schools and a new, more sensible, approach prevails.

Dividing adaptation into two types

Instead of "differentiating" for the pupils in your class, you are now expected to "adapt" for the pupils. And even further, you must distinguish between two types.

The first type is "pre-lesson adaptation". This is where a pupil in your class has a specific need, which requires a specific type of adaptation that requires pre-lesson planning. An example will be if you are to use a physical resource which a sight-impaired pupil cannot see. You review each lesson you are to teach them, and you arrange for larger versions to be created, if necessary (some sight-impaired pupils use magnification technology to assist them, but you would still need to evaluate each resource before the lesson is taught).

The second type is "in-lesson adaptation". This is when you are able to adapt a lesson at the moment to help support a pupil. This is a very strong and common strategy. For example, you might set up an independent task and then, once they begin the task, you would circulate around the class, adapting the task to make it easier or harder if this is necessary. You do not know you will need to adapt until you see the need emerge in-lesson. You will have one task for the entire class and then scaffold in the support or stretch as is necessary. If a pupil cannot access the task at all (e.g., an EAL pupil with very little English) then this would have been a pre-lesson adaptation, and you would have created the adaptation already.

You can see that, as a profession, we are gradually shifting towards adaptive learning – a more holistic approach that seeks to meet the needs of all pupils through responsive teaching strategies rather than segregated tasks or resources. In addition, it requires challenge to be at the heart of all learning. Pupils need to be stretched regardless of their demographic. What is important is that they are finding the work quite hard – not too hard and not too easy. This shift is a far more inclusive environment. It challenges the idea that some pupils require "easier" work and instead focuses on providing support and scaffolding that allows all pupils to engage with the same high-level content.

The reality is every pupil has some kind of need at any point of a lesson and in any subject. We must be thinking about all our pupils, not just some pupils, and we need to adapt to them all. This can lead to really very nuanced adaptations. For example, English teachers have to consider the narratives that they are presenting to pupils within the literary texts that they are teaching and whether such narratives are challenging or reinforcing ideas that their pupils have met elsewhere in their lives. If pupils only ever study texts where women are weak, and victims, whilst men are violent and heroes, then that does not challenge the stereotypes a pupil has experienced. Escalating that idea, you begin to see that people of colour, disability, poverty and special educational need can all be heroes or villains equally, but if pupils do not see this in the literature, they study, then they will not engage with the texts in the same way as some of their peers. In this way, we can see that adaptive learning supports the development of an aspirational mindset in pupils. When pupils are consistently exposed to high expectations and challenging content, they are more likely to develop resilience and a belief in their ability to improve through effort. By contrast, differentiated "easier" learning can inadvertently signal to pupils that they are not capable of engaging with more complex material, thus reinforcing negative mindsets and limiting their potential.

Lastly, adaptive learning aligns with the principles of equity in education, which are fairly widespread in secondary schools in England. It acknowledges that while pupils may have different starting points, they should all have the opportunity to achieve the same high outcomes. This is particularly important for pupils with SEND, who, under a differentiated model, might have been given less challenging work or excluded from certain activities altogether. Adaptive learning ensures that these pupils are not only included in all aspects of the curriculum but are also supported to achieve aspirational goals or aims

This shift in practice may well be in contrast to that which you have learned at your previous school. It might have been you were expected to show "differentiation" as part of a scrutiny programme. Even though it is quite an out-of-date idea, that does not mean it is not still done in some schools. If that is the case, then you must move away from the idea that different pupils need fundamentally different tasks and instead embrace the challenge of creating lessons that are accessible and challenging for all.

Formative assessment

Formative assessment plays a critical role in adaptive learning. By regularly assessing pupils' understanding and progress, you can identify where additional support or challenge is needed and adapt your teaching accordingly. Effective formative assessment goes beyond simple quizzes or tests; it involves ongoing detailed observation (through regular circulation), questioning and dialogue with pupils. You might use strategies such as exit tickets, where pupils write down what they have learned at the end of a lesson, or think-pair-share activities, where pupils discuss their ideas with a partner before sharing them with the class. If you are to adapt to your pupils, then you must have fine detail of when and where they need adaptation to, scaffold, support or stretch them.

Scaffolding and support for SEND pupils

Pupils with SEN or disability sometimes require additional support to access the curriculum and achieve high outcomes. In an adaptive learning environment, this support is provided, as set out in this section, through scaffolding rather than through differentiated tasks. Scaffolding involves breaking down complex tasks into smaller, more manageable steps, perhaps through worked-examples (which can help all pupils not just SEN) and providing temporary support until the pupil is able to complete the task independently. At the point they no longer need support, it is vital that the pupil is then weaned off the support. For example, common writing frames such as Point, Evidence and Explain (PEE) are helpful to weak writers who find writing whole paragraphs challenging. However, it is the teacher who is weak if they either use the writing frame with all pupils in the class or fail to wean the pupils off the writing frame once their ability to write well-constructed paragraphs has improved.

One key area of pre-lesson adaptation is about making lesson content or key vocabulary available in advance. Not just to the pupils, but to their parents or guardians and, if there is one, the teaching assistant who supports pupils in your lessons. Do not think it is you alone that is responsible for a pupil's learning content. They themselves, technology, teaching assistants and their extended family (and privately sourced tutors) will all play a part in the learning of content – and this means that they need to know what is coming up and especially if their SEND means they occasionally miss lessons. Knowing what they are going to miss enables them to ensure that learning can continue in a sequential form.

Building a classroom culture of inclusivity and high expectations

A successful classroom, drama studio, playing field, etc., that embraces adaptive learning depends not only on effective teaching strategies but also on a classroom culture that values inclusivity and high expectations for all pupils. This means fostering an environment where every pupil feels valued and supported, and where differences are seen as strengths rather than deficits. You, as a teacher in your school and MAT, play a key role in shaping this culture. You can set the tone by explicitly communicating your belief in every pupil's ability to succeed and by modelling inclusive behaviour. This will involve celebrating the diversity of experiences and perspectives within the classroom, encouraging collaboration and peer support and challenging any form of bias or discrimination that you see – whether in your lessons or in the corridors of your school. In addition to promoting inclusivity, you should consistently reinforce high expectations for all pupils. This means holding all pupils to the same standards of behaviour and academic performance, while providing the necessary support to help them meet those standards. By maintaining high expectations, you can help pupils develop a strong sense of self-efficacy and motivation, which, as we have repeatedly said in this book, are crucial for academic success. A pupil who has good metacognition around their learning will make strong progress in spite of a poor teacher as well as with a good teacher.

If working with SEND pupils is something new to you, or if your school has a greater diversity or number of SEND pupils than that which you have experienced before then it might be the case you need professional development in some of the areas of SEND. Your school or MAT will run workshops or programmes in which they look to develop their staff's ability to cater for the typical demographic for the school or MAT. That is part of good leadership and practice. They will certainly be monitoring data to ensure that good outcomes are being delivered by the school body and will take action across the school estate if outcomes for a subgroup are not being achieved. Stepping up and helping with this could be an opportunity for you, especially if you have knowledge or experience of SEND that you can bring to the school or MAT. Importantly, professional development should be seen as an ongoing process rather than a one-off thing. As you become more familiar with adaptive learning, you should continue experimenting with new strategies and reflect on their effectiveness. If working with SEND pupils is one of your strengths, then do look for opportunities to share this with the wider school or MAT staff.

Moving from differentiation to adaptation

The transition from differentiated to adaptive learning is a crucial step, for secondary schools in England, towards creating a more equitable education system for pupils from all demographics. By focusing on inclusive, responsive teaching strategies that meet the needs of all pupils, you can help ensure that every child has the opportunity to achieve strong outcomes. This shift might require a rethinking of traditional approaches to teaching from you, as well as a commitment to ongoing professional development and collaboration, and you should look to deliver this.

Ultimately, the goal of adaptive teaching is not just to support pupils with SEND or those who struggle academically, but to create a learning environment where every pupil can thrive. In doing so, we move closer to achieving an education system where inequalities do not lead to the division in outcomes that we currently have. As a teacher in the profession of teachers for secondary schools in England, you can play your part in achieving that outcome.

Mock examinations

This section outlines how to run mock examinations and use the data generated from them to improve outcomes. Running mock exams and analysing the resulting data is a specialist aspect of secondary teaching. It is likely that this will be the first of two sets of mock examinations for Year 11 and Year 13 pupils. Here, we will explore how to manage the deployment of examinations, the use of exam papers, assessment and moderation, as well as how to effectively use exam data to enhance pupil performance. We will also address the challenges of managing the workload during assessment periods and offer advice on how to navigate this successfully.

Choosing and preparing exam questions

The selection of exam questions is typically managed by the head of the department. However, it is wise to try and ascertain which questions they plan to use. This is important for several reasons. Firstly, you do not want to risk using the same questions in class three weeks before the mock exam. Additionally, there may be certain sources in History or specific texts in English that are too familiar to your pupils. While these might not appear in the actual June/July exams, if they come up in the mock, pupils might gain a false sense of their ability, thinking they are prepared when, in fact, they are not. If you plan to use a past exam paper, which many are available online, be mindful that pupils may also have access to them. This highlights the need for secrecy and ensuring that the mock exam remains a fair and unpredictable challenge for pupils.

Managing time and revision support

Effective time management is crucial when preparing for mocks, both in lessons and outside them. You must ensure that pupils have enough support in terms of revision materials, such as PowerPoint slides, revision sheets or feedback from previous exam questions. This support should ideally begin from the October half-term. Some pupils might have demonstrated a good grasp of exam techniques throughout the year, but they may perform differently under actual exam conditions. Remember, the mocks will only test the units that have been taught up until that point, so pupils will not be assessed on content they have not yet covered, such as units taught after the Christmas holidays.

It is also important to make sure pupils are clear on the exam question format and expectations. This could have been gauged in previous months or through earlier assessments. Understanding the specific techniques and criteria required to answer different question types is essential. For example, if the exam is for the English language, pupils must understand the skills needed to answer both 8-mark and 12-mark questions. Similarly, in Geography, if pupils are required to refer to a case study in question 3, they need to know this in advance so they can prepare accordingly.

The purpose of mock exams

The purpose of mock exams is not to catch pupils out, but rather to support your professional judgement in preparing effective interventions. The mocks provide insight into how pupils handle the pressure of exam conditions, how well they can answer questions within a time limit, and where they need additional support. For instance, if a large proportion of pupils struggle with a particular topic in Maths, such as trigonometry in Section A, this should inform the interventions you put in place. Similarly, if many pupils are unable to complete the final 16-mark question in History or English, this suggests that time management skills need to be developed further. Mock exams should, therefore, be viewed as an opportunity to identify areas for improvement and to prepare targeted support strategies.

Post-Examination tasks and managing workload

After the mock exams, you will be expected to mark the papers and submit data. This is likely to be required either before or just after the Christmas holidays, so it is important to plan your time effectively to ensure you can complete this work without compromising your holiday time. To manage this, it is helpful to establish a clear marking schedule well in advance and allocate specific times for grading and data input. This will help you to avoid feeling overwhelmed by the workload and ensure that the process is as smooth and efficient as possible. Some schools will want question-by-question data as this is the level of data which is provided in national examinations. Do not underestimate how long it takes to enter such data.

The data generated from mock exams will provide you with valuable insights into your pupils' strengths and areas for improvement. By analysing this data carefully, you will be able to tailor your teaching to meet the specific needs of your pupils and help them achieve better outcomes in their final exams. Through thoughtful intervention and a focus on exam technique, you can guide your pupils toward success, making the most of mock exam data to inform your practice.

Last day for resignations to start work after easter

This section provides essential guidance for teachers in England on applying for jobs, understanding resignation deadlines, and navigating employment-related decisions. It aligns with the principles outlined in the Burgundy Book, ensuring compliance with standard practices. You can read this guidance by googling the term "burgundy book". The Burgundy Book is a handbook setting out the conditions of service for schoolteachers in England and Wales. Its main provisions relate to notice periods, sick leave and pay and maternity leave and pay. Teachers must give two months' notice at all times, except for the final term in which the notice is three months.

To start with, if you feel that the school is not for you or that you don't like your line manager or the pupils may not be responding well to your teaching methods, these are all very common. Just remember that people will retire, get promoted or leave, so if it is personal, that is the issue, this may change. If the school is mainly ok and you feel you can work there, think long and hard, have some deeper reflections and ask yourself if there might be opportunities yet.

However, if you do wish to leave, then remember the following. As with the previous section during your time at your current school, whether you have been there for 4 months or 14 years, there is a cut-off of when to resign, in order for you to wish to leave by March or April, depending on when Easter is. You need two months of notice and starting a new role in the third term, the summer term, is slightly tricky because it is likely there are not two months between the end of February half term and the start of the summer term. You will need headteacher's permission to serve a slightly shorter notice. In principle, all headteachers are aware of this rule and are, in general, supportive of you giving notice by mid-February and starting a new role.

There are a few things that one has to consider before submitting the resignation to HR and having a conversation with the head/principal. Firstly, you should seek out sound advice from your line manager or others whom you trust about your feelings. Remember, some may feel the same as you, or have some similar experiences, but for them it is fine to carry on. They may seek to put a positive spin on your negative experiences and deflate your reasons for leaving.

Secondly, if you feel you do not wish to work beyond March/April and would like to start the spring in new employment, then you should consider how you wish to exit and the need to exercise strategic diplomacy, as you will need a reference. Although a reference is usually not overtly negative in its summative language, the reference provider may simply be factual and that in itself can speak volumes to a hiring headteacher.

January 18 days

Introduction

January brings a fresh start with a focus on safeguarding and the use of technology in teaching. This chapter highlights the importance of identifying potential safeguarding issues, especially after the Christmas break, and re-establishing routines to prevent discipline issues. It also explores how to integrate new technology into the classroom, using the start of a new term to experiment with innovative teaching methods.

Safeguarding

This section of the chapter explores how to support pupils who may increasingly demonstrate safeguarding risks, even after the designated safeguarding lead (DSL) has been informed. It provides guidance on identifying potential issues that may arise when pupils have been away from school for an extended period, such as two weeks during the Christmas break. Some pupils may have faced hardships during this time and will need additional support. The section also highlights the importance of re-establishing routines to prevent discipline issues, with a particular focus on expected behaviour, work ethic, and dress code.

Identifying potential safeguarding issues

As you and your colleagues return to teaching after the Christmas break, it is crucial to recognise that safeguarding becomes an even more important part of your daily responsibilities. While the break may have been a time of relaxation and rest for many, for some pupils, it can be a challenging and unstable period. Pupils who rely on regular school meals, a safe space to study, and access to supportive adults may have encountered difficulties during this time. Even if the DSL has been informed of such issues, it remains essential for you to stay vigilant and proactive in supporting these pupils as they reintegrate into the school environment.

In the first days following the break, it is important to remain attuned to any subtle signs that a pupil may be experiencing difficulties. You should be alert to changes in behaviour, appearance or attitude. While it is important to continue following the school's behaviour policy, you should also consider whether there might be underlying issues affecting a pupil's behaviour. For example, a pupil might appear unusually withdrawn, agitated or distracted, which could signal that they are struggling with something beyond the classroom.

It is crucial to address any concerns promptly. Do not hesitate to consult with other members of staff or the DSL, as they may have additional information or context that you do not. Remember that the DSL relies on your vigilance in spotting these indicators, so your observations can play a key role in ensuring that pupils receive the support they need.

Re-establishing routines for stability

Beyond identifying safeguarding concerns, re-establishing regular routines is vital for all pupils, as it creates a sense of normality and security. The return to school after a break can be disruptive, and without clear expectations, discipline issues may arise. By reinforcing the school's established routines – such as punctuality, dress code, how pupils enter the room and how they get ready for lesson starts or undertake opening tasks – you help set a positive tone for the term ahead.

It is also important to remind pupils of the behaviour standards and academic expectations, emphasising that these expectations will be consistently upheld. Even if pupils have just returned from a break, it is essential to make clear that the same level of discipline and commitment to work will be expected from them. This helps to re-establish structure and security, which is particularly important for those who may have experienced instability during the break.

Providing a safe and structured environment

To summarise, all pupils, whether they are aware of it or not, will benefit from a return to a tightly structured learning environment. This environment offers them safety, the assurance of meals regardless of their financial situation and the support of adults who genuinely care about their well-being. For many pupils, the return to school will provide a sense of relief and stability, particularly if they have faced difficulties during the break.

It is not uncommon for pupils to have a challenging time after a holiday, whether due to safeguarding concerns or personal reasons, such as having to divide their time between two different families over Christmas. In these cases, your role as a safe and dependable adult is invaluable. By offering a reliable and fair structure, you provide the consistency and support that these pupils may need to thrive.

By recognising the signs of difficulty, being proactive in offering support, and re-establishing routines, you will help pupils navigate the challenges that may arise after the break. Your attentiveness can make a significant difference in their well-being and academic success, ensuring that they feel safe and supported as they continue their learning journey. This environment you and your school provide will be safe, provide them with food whether they can afford it or not and seek to ensure that they are supported throughout their day-to-day living by adults who have their best interests at heart. It is often the case that this period can sometimes be challenging as teachers deal with the aftermath of their pupils having a difficult time, sometimes for safeguarding reasons and sometimes for other reasons such as trying to have Christmas with two different families. Being that safe and dependable person who offers reliable and fair structure and support can be just what they all need.

The use of technology in teaching

This section of the chapter will support the use of technology in teaching. As technology is a modality through which learning takes place the section will explore how the beginning of the January term is a good place to deploy the latest methods. Teachers will know the class, have rehearsed the technology and can use the start of a new topic to explore the new practice.

Embracing the new in the January term

In recent years, the role of technology in education has rapidly evolved, transforming from a supplemental tool into an essential part of secondary classroom teaching and learning. Why, then, is this section in January? Well, unlike the pre-existing systems and technology you had to learn at the start of the academic year, this is a great time for experimenting.

January provides a fresh start, in the academic year, where both pupils can work together as they experience new content and new ways of learning. After a term of establishing relationships and classroom routines, teachers can introduce innovative technology without the distractions and disruptions that might occur at the very beginning of the school year. It is a time when teachers have good knowledge of what their pupils are capable of, and thus it enables them to adapt the use of technology to enhance the learning process.

Implementing new technology-based methods of teaching and learning during this time allows for experimentation and refinement. You can test how your pupils respond to different tools and approaches, giving you the flexibility to adjust without losing the hard-won routines and discipline of the classroom. By starting fresh with a new topic, pupils also view the integration of new learning technology as a natural part of the learning process, rather than a sudden shift in the middle of a familiar routine. The key here is that technology, when used effectively, is not just a replacement for traditional methods – like switching a whiteboard for an interactive version – it becomes a dynamic way to deepen learning.

Moving beyond the interactive whiteboard

Too often, when we talk about the use of technology in the classroom, we limit the conversation to basic tools like interactive whiteboards or projectors. While these can certainly be useful, they barely scratch the surface of what modern technology can offer in enhancing both teaching and learning. It is important to move beyond the simplistic substitution of old tools with their digital counterparts and start thinking about how to use technology to open new avenues for exploration and understanding. For example, consider the use of real-world technology to make classroom learning more relevant. In Geography, teachers can use interactive tools to give pupils a hands-on understanding of how geographic factors influence human settlement, property value and urban planning. This goes far beyond pointing at a map – pupils can engage with live data, compare locations in real-time, and understand the socio-economic and environmental factors shaping our world today. Learning to use real-life data and tools is an essential part of not just learning a topic and subject, but inspiring epistemic curiosity. As a secondary teacher, you want your pupils to be exploring your subject of their own volition. You want them to opt into your subject at GCSE and A level and go on to enter the employment market in your area, perhaps as through an apprenticeship route, or alternatively to read your subject or a related counterpart at university. Technology can help you, as a teacher, achieve that aim by brokering your pupils to how your subject is using technology to view data and content within your subject.

Technology across the curriculum

Whilst technology may seem like a natural fit for subjects like Geography or Design and Technology, its application spans across other subjects – including in less obvious areas like PE and History. The key is in using technology not as a novelty but as a tool for deeper engagement and learning. In PE, technology can be used to track physical activity, measure progress and even simulate athletic training scenarios. For example, wearable fitness trackers allow pupils to monitor their heart rate, distance travelled and calories burned during exercise, giving them a more scientific understanding of physical fitness. Teachers can use apps and software to assess progress over time, offering personalised feedback that encourages pupils to set and meet fitness goals beyond that they are learning in lessons. They can begin to see that PE is not just a subject to be studied, but a lifestyle to be maintained. Similarly, in History, technology can bring the past to life in ways that traditional textbooks cannot. Virtual reality (VR) or augmented reality (AR) allows pupils to experience historical events and places first-hand. Imagine pupils walking through ancient Rome, exploring medieval castles, or witnessing key moments in History through immersive experiences. These technologies make history not just something to be learned but something to be experienced, fostering a deeper connection to the subject matter. You will see your pupils' interest in these areas being transformed, especially if they had only had limited experiences before.

Even in a computer room setting (although these are very much being phased out and being replaced with mobile devices), the possibilities are vast. Whether it is for English, Maths or Science, using the computer lab effectively can turn a passive learning environment into an interactive one. In Maths, for example, pupils can use software to create practical examples of complex equations and functions, or to simulate real-world scenarios where Maths is applied – such as engineering or architectural projects. In English, pupils can collaborate on documents asynchronously with their fellow pupils, which mimics how co-construction of written texts in work environments takes place. At the moment, in key stage four, such practice does not exist due to the nature of the examination at GCSE, but it should certainly be possible at key stage three.

The importance of technological integration

While it is easy to get excited about the possibilities that technology offers, it is important to remember that purposeful integration is the key to success. Technology should not be used for its own sake – it should serve a clear pedagogical purpose. As a teacher, you need to consider how each tool enhances learning, supports your pupils' understanding of the curriculum and encourages long-term outcomes like critical thinking, creativity and collaboration.

To achieve this, it is important to plan carefully. You should start by identifying the learning outcomes you want to achieve and then select the technology that best supports those outcomes. For example, if the goal is for pupils to understand geographic factors in urban development, interactive maps and real-time data might be the best tools. If the goal is to encourage collaboration and communication in an English class, using shared documents could be more appropriate. Be aware, however, that in secondary schools in England there has been a direct shift away from pupils using their smartphones in class. This is because it leads to too many behavioural issues, even when strictly controlled. It is likely that if pupils are to use mobile devices in your teaching, then they are devices provided by your school. Some schools now offer Chromebooks to all pupils and some schools heavily restrict access to any technology by pupils whatsoever. It really depends on the vision and ideological opinions of the leadership in the school and MAT as to whether technology plays a central role in learning within your school.

Preparing for a tech-savvy future

The use of technology in teaching is not just about keeping up with the times – it is about preparing pupils for a future where digital literacy is essential. By integrating technology in meaningful ways, teachers can create more engaging, relevant and effective learning experiences for their pupils. Whether through online tools, real-world applications, or immersive virtual experiences, technology offers endless opportunities to enhance the way we teach and learn.

As the January term begins, you have a unique opportunity to explore these tools and methods, experimenting with new practices that can bring their subjects to life. The future of education is digital, and those of you who embrace the possibilities of technology in your teaching will be best positioned to help your pupils succeed in a rapidly changing world.

February 18 days

Introduction

In February, the focus is on rebuilding rapport with pupils after the holidays and incorporating creativity into your teaching. This chapter provides strategies for mending strained relationships and engaging pupils through creative teaching methods. It also discusses the benefits of school trips, offering practical advice on logistics and safeguarding to ensure successful and enriching experiences for pupils.

Rebuilding rapport post-holidays

This section of the chapter focuses on how to rebuild and strengthen relationships between teachers and pupils that may have become strained. It addresses how various factors, such as a lack of enthusiasm for the subject, poor behaviour or personality clashes, can negatively impact the teacher-pupil dynamic, making lessons after a school holiday (whether it be half-term, Christmas, or Easter) an opportunity to reset and start afresh. The section provides strategies for mending bridges, bringing pupils on side, and managing incidents that cause stress in order to restore a productive classroom environment.

Strained relationships

Every lesson presents a new opportunity for a teacher to do their job and teach their pupils, but this can be particularly challenging when working with pupils who are uncooperative. There are many reasons why a relationship between a teacher and a pupil may become strained. It could be a lack of enthusiasm for the subject, the time of day, previous negative encounters with the teacher, or personal issues the pupil is facing. As teachers, we have a duty to teach all the pupils in our classes, even when relationships feel difficult. It is important to remember that, as adults, we have the life experience and professional training to guide pupils in building better relationships, learning how to forgive and ultimately developing a more productive working dynamic.

Causes of strained relationships

There may be times when a class or individual pupils are uncooperative, leading to stress or anxiety for the teacher. It is important to approach these situations calmly and constructively. Seek to understand the root causes of the pupil's behaviour. If the issue is external, it is crucial not to take it personally. For example, a pupil may act out not just with you but with other colleagues as well. Recognising this can help to reduce your own stress, as it will remind you that the pupil's behaviour is not a reflection of your teaching. Understanding the broader context can help you approach the situation with empathy, and in turn, allow you to build a more amicable relationship with the pupil.

Impact on attainment

Just as in many aspects of life, if a pupil is happier and feels supported, their productivity and engagement in the classroom will improve. The same principle applies to their academic attainment. If pupils feel that they are being offered a fresh start after a break, this can have a positive impact on their motivation and performance. For example, if there is a new topic to begin after a holiday, this might inspire more enthusiasm in some pupils, while others may find it less engaging. In PE, for instance, a shift from individual sports to team sports might spark excitement in some pupils, while others may prefer the previous sports. Similarly, in Maths a pupil who excelled in the previous topic might find the new one more challenging. This is where it is essential for you as the teacher to maintain momentum from the previous term, providing continued support to ensure that every pupil can succeed, regardless of the challenges they face with new content.

It is also important to recognise that during the break, significant events may have occurred in the pupil's life or within their community. For example, national events, such as the 2024 riots in various parts of England, or personal events like the death of a family member or a sibling leaving for university, can affect a pupil's emotional state. Such events may make pupils feel more vulnerable or unsettled, which highlights the need for supportive and understanding teachers during this time.

Tips for rebuilding relationships after the February half-term

1. **Be Positive When Greeting Pupils:** upon seeing the pupils in question, always approach them in a positive manner. A simple, non-intrusive greeting like, "Hi Jamie, how are you?" or "Hello Jamie, did you have a good break from school?" can help create an opportunity for positive interaction.

2. **Set Expectations Early:** once you are in the classroom, take the first few minutes of each lesson in the first week back to remind all pupils of the school's expectations and your own class rules. This helps to re-establish

continuity from the previous term and ensures that pupils understand what is expected of them.

3. **Avoid Referencing Past Issues:** to rebuild trust, avoid bringing up past conflicts or issues from the previous term. Make it clear to the pupils that each lesson is a new opportunity to do well and improve upon previous performance. This approach helps to create a sense of hope and possibility for the future.

4. **Liaise with Colleagues:** it is helpful to communicate with your colleagues about the expectations for pupils after the break. Some schools may require assessment feedback on the first day back, which could potentially lead to issues with pupils who performed poorly or exhibited behavioural problems in the previous term. Consulting with the Head of Department or Faculty will ensure you are aligned with school-specific expectations and can plan accordingly.

By following these strategies, you can help rebuild and strengthen your relationships with pupils after a break, fostering a positive and productive classroom environment. This not only improves the teacher-pupil dynamic but can also lead to better academic outcomes, as pupils feel more supported and engaged in their learning.

Creative teaching

This section will cover the need for creativity in teaching in order to find fulfilment within the profession. It will explore how, throughout your teaching career, there will undoubtedly be times when pupils do not find the lesson, topic, or teaching method engaging. Creativity is one of the most powerful tools to counter this challenge. This section will demonstrate how accessing wider reading can provide ideas and examples of using role play, language, music, video production and art-based strategies to ensure pre-written schemes of learning are adapted to spark curiosity and engagement. It will also address the reluctance many teachers feel when adapting pre-existing planning, especially for GCSE classes, due to the content load and limited time. A range of examples from English, History and Science GCSE lessons will illustrate how adaptation can take place. Additionally, personal development strategies will be offered to encourage creativity, such as seeking support from colleagues and line managers to see the educational value of these adaptations. Finally, it will include practical exercises to help teachers, even those who do not consider themselves creative, to adapt lessons effectively.

Teaching is creative

Even though in the majority of schools you will be required to follow centralised planning, the opportunities to use imagination in your lessons are endless.

Unlike many other professions, such as medicine or law, creativity in teaching can be a bonus that many may not fully appreciate. For example, as a teacher, you will have undoubtedly encountered groans and disengagement from pupils dragging their feet to your lessons, particularly from new classes unfamiliar with your teaching style or whom have a preference for their previous teacher of your subject.

Unfortunately, it is easy for teachers to feel overwhelmed by the pressure to deliver content, which can lead to an overuse of instructional pedagogy such as comprehension tasks, direct instruction or copying information from PowerPoint slides. Yet, as adults, our engagement in training sessions or CPD often depends significantly on how the content is delivered. Why should pupils be any different? It is essential to consider how to make lessons engaging without compromising educational outcomes. By this, we mean your subject is already interesting and it does not need "events" to liven it up. What we mean is that you should seek to encourage epistemic curiosity in your subject so that your pupils appreciate how compelling your subject is. If you only teach to the examination and set that as the end purpose then your pupils will become uninspired. If you combine good outcomes with curiosity in your subject as an end objective then your pupils will consider continuing with your subject in their own time and in future study.

Do not despair if you feel you are not naturally creative or that your teaching style lacks flair. There are strategies that can transform even the most disengaged pupils into more enthusiastic participants in your lessons.

Strategies for creativity in lessons

The first step is to identify which part of the lesson can be delivered differently. This could be as simple as replacing traditional questioning methods with activities like having pupils write answers on sticky notes and posting them on the wall or using mini whiteboards to display their responses. Alternatively, you could use group work where pupils produce knowledge through discussion. Group work is tricky to do well, but high-quality teachers use precise strategies to ensure that the task is one that can only be done by a group (to that solo pupils cannot disengage) and also that there is clear structure to the work – agendas, timings, role cards and limiting time as a group all play a part in this.

Once you have pinpointed an area for creative adaptation, follow this four-step plan to ensure its success:

1. **Seek Advice from Experienced Colleagues:** ask your colleagues how they might approach a particular topic or activity. Their experiences can provide valuable insights and practical suggestions. For example, if you are teaching a challenging Year 9 group on a Tuesday morning, a colleague may have tried a creative approach that worked well with a similar class.

2. **Understand Your Pupils:** gauge the emotional maturity, responsibility and aptitude of the pupils involved. If you have reservations about their behaviour or capabilities, consider scaling back the level of creativity or providing scaffolding to support their engagement. For instance, if planning a debate, ensure pupils are prepared with the necessary knowledge and skills beforehand.

3. **Align Creativity with Learning Objectives:** creativity should enhance, not detract from, purposeful learning. For example, if you are using a video in a GCSE Geography lesson, ensure it is directly relevant to the exam content or the skills being developed.

4. **Prepare Pupils and Resources Thoroughly:** ensure preceding lessons provide the foundation for the creative activity. Resources should be readily available, and time management must be carefully planned. Clear instructions and behaviour management are essential to ensure the lesson runs smoothly and maintains focus.

Examples of creative approaches

Role play

Role play is a versatile tool that can be tailored to suit various subjects and topics. For a quick activity, you might ask pupils to articulate, as a specialist, a brief summary of the learning so far, outlining key points and arguments. For a more complex approach, pupils could work in groups to enact scenarios related to the topic. For example, in Geography, pupils might simulate a news report on the aftermath of a natural disaster, taking on roles such as journalists, emergency responders, and affected residents. This type of activity requires more planning and time, but can significantly enhance curiosity and understanding.

Language-based activities

Language can be a powerful tool for engaging pupils and reinforcing learning. Acronyms, like BODMAS in Maths, are a simple way to support memory. Alternatively, you could challenge pupils to summarise a topic in progressively fewer words – first in a paragraph, then in a sentence, and finally in just three key words. This technique can be applied across subjects to encourage concise thinking and mastery of key concepts.

Music and media

Music and media can bring a creative dimension to lessons. For instance, pupils might create a short rap or song to explain a scientific process or historical event. Alternatively, you could use a video clip without sound, prompting pupils to create their own commentary or dialogue. For example, in Science, a clip showing the food chain could be narrated by pupils to reinforce their understanding of ecological processes.

Group work

Group-based activities can develop social skills, confidence and collaborative learning. When assigning group tasks, consider the balance of abilities within each group and provide clear objectives and timelines. For example, a group project in Business Studies might involve researching and presenting on the growth of a company, with each member assigned specific roles and responsibilities. Structured guidance ensures the activity remains focused and productive.

Building confidence in creativity

If you do not consider yourself a naturally creative teacher, start small. Introduce simple activities or tasks lasting just a few minutes every two to three weeks. Gradually expand your repertoire as your confidence grows. Over time, you will build a toolkit of creative strategies that will enrich your teaching and make lessons more engaging for your pupils.

The skiing trip and others, abroad

This section of the chapter will seek to offer alternative educational opportunities. February is a harsh month for weather in England, so it is often the right time to take a trip abroad. It is not unusual for schools in England to organise a trip during the half-term. This can be academically related or simply an enjoyable trip abroad to go skiing. It should not be underestimated – schools are in competition with each other in England and being able to organise and offer a wide range of trips as part of the curriculum is an important part of being a secondary teacher in England. This section of the chapter sets out sensible advice around logistics and safeguarding in trip organisation. Whilst some teachers will have never worked in a school offering such extra-curricular activities, being able to organise and offer these trips helps with their employability and so this chapter will be instrumental in supporting this.

Why undertake school trips abroad?

Imagine swapping the chilly February half-term for a snowy Alps village or the bustling streets of Rome. School trips abroad can be a fantastic adventure, both for you as a teacher and for your pupils. Beyond the excitement, these trips offer rich educational experiences that can't be replicated in a classroom. Whether you're exploring ancient ruins with your History class or hitting the slopes with a mix of pupils, these experiences not only deepen learning but can boost your own career prospects! A head interviewing a prospective teacher will be pleased to hear you have experience and confidence in organising international trips. This is because in today's competitive school environment, having a teacher who organises unique trips alongside the approved social media showcasing can make a big difference for your school. Make no mistake, schools and MATs have serious plans around

Why school trips make a difference

Here's the thing: learning doesn't automatically transfer from one setting to another. We, as teachers, know this well. Sociologist Pierre Bourdieu's idea of "transposable habitus" explains that skills picked up in one environment – like the classroom – may not stick when pupils find themselves in new situations. That is why trips abroad are so powerful. Take a pupil who has studied French for years but has only spoken it in a classroom. Their memories are of classroom-based role plays. When their teacher does retrieval practice with them, they will be retrieving a memory of being in a classroom. Now, compare that to them in France, ordering a latte in French. Very Emily in Paris! They will remember that moment, photo or video that moment, share that moment, and their confidence will grow as well as their love for speaking French. Plus, they will come back with a stronger skill set, ready to apply what they learned in different, real-world contexts.

Mastering the details: Logistics and safety first

Planning a trip abroad is not just about picking a destination and packing a bag. It is a logistical event where you are expected to think of everything: travel routes, accommodation and activities, not to mention emergency contacts, medical information and permissions. A thorough risk assessment is your best friend here. And when it comes to staffing, think ahead: make sure you have the right pupil-to-adult ratios and that your team of staff is clear on who is handling what. The more you plan, the smoother the trip and the more fun everyone will have. Teachers who are good at planning are the ones that organise great trips. Luckily, a hallmark of a great teacher is one who is good at organising and so we are blessed with lots of hyper-organised teachers in the profession. Even if that is not you, do not worry, with the help of some AI tools, you can ensure that you have a strong organised patina to all your organising. Modern teachers have to be AI literate. Before you undertake any large organisational task spend 60 seconds consulting AI because there is no escaping; that 60 seconds will change the way you approach the task.

Building trust and connection outside the classroom

One of the unexpected bonuses of school trips is how they help you and your pupils create a strong bond and relationship. Shared adventures – whether it is trekking through a new city trying to find the art gallery or trying an unfamiliar cuisine – build trust and shared memories that can really last back in the classroom. After the winter break, for example, chatting with pupils about their memories of the trip or favourite parts of the experience can really enable you to take the conversation into a place where you begin to broker a lifelong love of your subject and the opportunities that exist for those interested in developing and pursuing further opportunities. Even a simple trip skiing enables you as a teacher to talk about sandwich courses at university where they can experience being in a university in another country for a year of their study.

It is important for your pupils to see that they can view their current lives through the lens of their school trip, especially if it was a trip which involved experiencing a different culture. Get them to reflect, perhaps in a graphic journal or similar, on the cultural differences they observed and to bring their other subjects into their observations. If they study art, they can sketch architecture, if they study food technology, they can capture food differences. The more your pupils can connect the trip to the subjects that they are studying, then the more meaningful the trip becomes. If you get it right, your pupils will come back from the trip with a new lens through which to view their everyday life and experiences. It might just be the catalyst to transform them as they move through their teenage years into early adulthood.

Boosting your career with every trip

Leading a successful school trip does not just earn you a few appreciation cards from pupils and parents, it demonstrates your skills in organisation, leadership and problem-solving – all highly desirable traits in the teaching world. Plus, being known as the teacher who successfully leads safe, but exciting school trips adds a layer to your CV, showing that you are proactive, versatile and can inspire pupils beyond the classroom. And, as you will soon realise, these skills will help you progress up the teaching career ladder or move to another more desirable school if that is what you want to do.

Taking the leap

Organising a school trip abroad may feel daunting, but it is a challenge well worth taking on. With every passport check and itinerary tweak, you are building experiences that will leave a lasting impact on pupils and offer you genuine career growth opportunities. Embrace the adventure, trust your planning and dive in!

A note on accessibility: Supporting all pupils

While school trips abroad offer invaluable experiences, it is essential to recognise that not every pupil or school can participate in such trips. For some families, the cost is simply out of reach. As teachers, we need to be sensitive to this reality and work toward inclusivity. One way to approach this is by exploring funding options or considering sponsorships and fundraising initiatives that can help reduce costs. The goal is to ensure every pupil feels valued and engaged, regardless of their ability to join. By acknowledging and addressing these disparities, we help create a more equitable learning environment. Just because some pupils cannot afford a trip, it does not mean no schools should organise trips abroad or otherwise. Rather, we should be as inclusive as possible. It may be that instead of school trips abroad you need to consider the opposite type of support such as food parcels and extended pastoral care. This next section will give you a good idea of how to go about this.

Food parcels and extended pastoral care

This chapter will outline how some schools ensure their pupils achieve a good education by extending their pastoral care offer to ensure basic needs such as food and access to clean clothing and bedding are available. Further advice regarding recent entries to the country and brokering support facilities will be outlined and in general this chapter will enable teachers to understand the needs of schools which are in deprived areas or areas which have seen a recent influx in contrasting pupil demographics.

There is a broad range of socio-economic conditions represented within the pupil body in many schools. Your school may have a significant or a small number of pupils who are living in poverty. No child should have their socio-economic status – an aspect entirely beyond their control – used as an explanation or justification for poor academic attainment or, more importantly, unhappiness at school. Therefore, if your school has pupils who require additional help, the nature of teaching compels one to do what is possible to assist. While this issue is far too vast for a single class teacher or even a school to resolve entirely, there are practical steps that can be taken to make the lives of these pupils a little better.

School duty and socio-economic challenges

Some pupils may come from families where significant life events, such as parental divorce, have drastically altered their economic circumstances. These abrupt changes can create difficulties in understanding their new socio-economic reality and can disrupt their relationship with learning. Such challenges may manifest in a variety of ways, requiring the school community to provide targeted support.

Many schools will have pupils from extremely deprived socio-economic backgrounds. These children often need support that extends beyond standard provisions like breakfast clubs. For instance, they may lack adequate sanitation facilities at home and require assistance with dental care, bathing, or menstruation management. Although initiatives like the Pupil Premium fund are designed to help, they are often insufficient and additional financial resources may need to be sought. School leaders frequently go to great lengths to support these pupils, but the needs can outstrip available funding, particularly in schools serving disadvantaged communities.

Practical strategies for teachers

While systemic issues require broader solutions, individual teachers can take steps to support pupils facing socio-economic challenges. These include:

Avoid publicly highlighting a pupil's poverty, as this can be condescending and counterproductive. Instead, bring concerns discreetly to the safeguarding lead or pastoral team. This ensures the issue is addressed appropriately while preserving the pupil's dignity.

Seek help for issues beyond your expertise. For example, if you notice a pupil struggling with poor hygiene due to a lack of resources, involve the safeguarding team or other support mechanisms. This might include addressing menstruation-related needs or finding discreet ways to help with hygiene issues.

In cases of poor body odour, consider practical, non-stigmatising solutions, such as opening windows for ventilation or using an asthma-friendly air freshener. Other pupils may not always be empathetic and might use such situations as an opportunity for bullying. Your actions can help create a more inclusive and respectful environment.

Handle situations involving Pupil Premium or Free School Meals pupils with sensitivity. For example, during school trips or at lunchtime, ensure that these pupils receive their entitlement discreetly to avoid drawing attention to their circumstances. This approach fosters respect and helps reduce any anxiety or stigma the pupils might feel.

Hunger and its impact on learning

Hunger significantly impairs a pupil's ability to concentrate and engage with their lessons. Supporting pupils who come to school hungry is essential, not only as a fundamental safeguarding responsibility but also as a means of enabling them to reach their potential. Schools must continue to prioritise initiatives that address hunger and ensure that all pupils are adequately nourished during the school day.

By taking these steps, teachers can play a vital role in supporting pupils from disadvantaged backgrounds. While the broader issues of poverty and inequality require systemic solutions, individual actions can have a meaningful and positive impact on the lives of the pupils we serve.

March 20 days

Introduction

March is all about options evenings and building confidence in your professionalism. This chapter offers advice on promoting your subject to pupils and parents, ensuring healthy numbers for GCSE or A-level selections. It also addresses imposter syndrome, providing strategies for building confidence and developing a personalised career plan. The goal is to help you feel empowered and assertive in your role.

Options evenings

This section will enable teachers to strategise to enhance their subject's popularity and perceived importance (and ensure that their subject is selected in healthy numbers at GCSE or A level if it is not a compulsory subject). It will give advice about the marketing of a subject, how it is vital and getting pupils to choose your subject at GCSE or A level is important. The section will cover how schools have options evenings consisting of marketing opportunities consisting of activities such as digital presentations to be used online, social media posts, taster sessions, videos, posters and stalls with resources and materials. It will explore methods of building interest in your subject from as early as Year 7 with a range of strategies and examples used. It will cover growing your subject from small provision to large provision if you are a small department, such as music or religious education.

Building rapport and making an impression at Key Stage 3

In Key Stage 3, especially in schools that teach KS3 all the way until the end of Year 9, there are three years to build a strong rapport with pupils and showcase the value and enjoyment of your subject before the seriousness of GCSEs arrives. For core subjects such as Maths and English, this process is naturally embedded, as pupils will continue with these throughout their schooling. However, for optional subjects, those in the blocks from which pupils choose their GCSE options, this period is vital. From Year 7 onwards, there is an implicit and steady "sales pitch" taking place. You must view each pupil as a potential "customer" of your subject, understanding that their choices will shape your class composition in the years to come.

Not all recruitment will necessarily align with your ideal teaching scenario. Some pupils will be motivated and engaged, offering substantial returns for your effort, while others may be less inclined to contribute positively. It is essential to approach this reality with a balance of enthusiasm and pragmatism.

The impact of curiosity on pupil choices

Pupils form an understanding of your pedagogical approach over time. This includes the methods you use, the consistency of your teaching and the variety you bring to lessons. For example, a Modern Foreign Languages teacher who frequently utilises small-group work may appeal to some pupils but alienate others who prefer independent study. Similarly, in History, a method requiring every pupil to read aloud in class may discourage those who are less confident in speaking publicly. Alternatively, a classroom with significant background noise may unsettle pupils who thrive in quieter, more focused environments.

These preferences, alongside the clarity of subject content and assessment expectations, play a significant role in a pupil's decision to choose your subject. Additionally, some pupils may select a subject based on the teacher, only to be taught by someone else later. For this reason, it is critical to ensure that the subject itself, not merely your personality or teaching style, is the primary draw.

Preparing for options evenings: The stall and presentation

The stall or table

The options evening is a crucial opportunity to sell your subject to pupils and their parents. Whether your school hosts all subjects in a single hall or spreads them across classrooms, your stall is the centrepiece of your presentation. To create a successful stall, you should consider the following:

1. **Content:** decide what will go on the stall. Will you showcase textbooks, exercise books, or other technological resources? Be selective – choose a few compelling items to display and open these to particularly engaging pages. In Science, diagrams of the liver's inner workings or the physics of gravity could captivate pupils' curiosity.

2. **Interaction:** consider how much space you will leave for browsing and whether you will actively guide discussions or allow parents and pupils to explore independently.

3. **Hooks:** ensure your stall stands out. This might include visual elements such as models, colourful displays or interactive materials. Aim to stimulate curiosity and draw in even the most reluctant visitors.

The room

If your options event is held in a classroom or department-specific area, ensure that the room enhances, rather than detracts from, your subject's appeal. Begin by addressing practical concerns:

- Cleanliness: ensure the room is free of graffiti and clutter, with movable furniture and personal items out of sight.
- Ventilation: keep the room well-aired to avoid unpleasant odours, which can be off-putting for visitors.
- Layout: arrange the space to allow free movement, accommodating the flow of visitors.
- Displays: update noticeboards with fresh, visually appealing materials that reflect current pupils' work and subject achievements.

Creating the right atmosphere

To foster a welcoming and engaging environment, select a range of helpful pupils to assist on the evening. Choose those who are personable and enthusiastic about the subject rather than just well-behaved. Assign specific tasks to these helpers to ensure they remain focused and contribute positively to the event.

Consider using a PowerPoint presentation on a loop to provide additional information. A series of 40 slides, each displayed for 5–10 seconds, can offer a snapshot of your subject's highlights without overwhelming visitors. Keep the content simple and visually appealing to avoid cognitive overload.

It is also advisable to wear fresh, professional attire for the evening. Clothing worn during the school day may appear creased or less polished, detracting from the professional image you aim to project.

Activities and engagement

Incorporating interactive activities can make your subject more memorable and engaging. Examples include:

- In History, allow pupils to handle replica artefacts and match them to their origins, such as trade goods from the British Empire.
- In Drama, challenge visitors to match famous quotes to scenes from well-known plays.

- In Business Studies or Economics, simulate stock market investments using live data and monopoly money.

Addressing practical concerns

Be honest about the workload and requirements of your subject. For example, product design pupils may need to maintain a portfolio, demanding a high level of independence. Highlighting links to industry and employment can also reassure parents who question the long-term value of subjects like History or Music.

Professional conduct

Throughout the evening, maintain a professional and approachable demeanour. Avoid distractions such as checking emails or engaging with your phone. Plan short breaks for refreshments or rest, but ensure that your stall remains staffed and inviting. Finally, if you encounter parents or pupils whom you know personally, maintain a professional tone while being friendly and welcoming.

By preparing thoroughly and engaging effectively, you can make a compelling case for your subject, leaving a lasting impression on pupils and their families.

Building confidence in your professionalism

This section will approach the contemporary topic of negativity and emergence of imposter syndrome where sometimes teachers do not feel able or knowledgeable enough to do their job. It will outline the support available in extinguishing this through access to wider reading, self-study and through interaction with subject communities. The section will revisit the notion that evidence-informed teachers are still able to adapt within a centralised provision and develop a positive "can do" and "will do" mentality. Finally, this section will focus on fallibility and the acceptance that no teacher is the fountain of all knowledge, but that teachers have the ability to become very knowledgeable over their career.

Building confidence as a teacher

After successfully navigating a challenging interview process, it is crucial to remember one vital truth: the school's leadership team chose you because they have confidence in your abilities. This belief in your potential is the foundation of your role as a teacher. It is especially important to hold onto this fact during moments when you may doubt your confidence and passion for the profession or role.

Cultivating confidence

It is entirely natural to occasionally feel that you are not performing at your best or that there is room for improvement. Reflection and a desire to enhance your practice are not indicators of failure but rather signs of a committed and conscientious teacher. In these moments, it is essential to focus on the positives in your practice.

Consider the successes you have already achieved, such as lessons that were well-received by pupils, activities that sparked engagement and progression, or even something as simple as a well-structured lesson that ran smoothly. Think about the conversations you have had with pupils, the feedback you have received from colleagues, and the documented outcomes of your work – such as improved assessment results, increased attendance of reluctant pupils or the gradual development of confidence and participation in your classroom.

Here are some strategies to help maintain your confidence as a teacher:

1. **Keep a Personal Record:** document the highlights of each term. Note moments that made you proud or brought a smile to your face. This could include a successful lesson, a kind comment from a pupil, or evidence of progress in your class. These reflections are subjective and personal – nobody can challenge your view of your own achievements.

2. **Seek Feedback:** invite a colleague to observe a specific part of your lesson for 10–15 minutes and provide constructive feedback. This focused observation can highlight your strengths and remind you of your effectiveness, especially during challenging times.

3. **Focus on Your Journey:** teaching is not a competition. Each teacher is on their own path, and as long as you are working within the professional standards, you are progressing. Avoid comparing yourself to others and concentrate on your growth.

Addressing imposter syndrome

If you are teaching, then you are a qualified teacher – there is no need to prove otherwise. Your qualifications, experience and presence in the classroom are all evidence of your legitimacy. Teaching is a role defined by action, and every lesson you deliver is a testament to your ability to inspire, educate and empower pupils.

Building confidence often involves identifying personal anchors that reinforce your sense of professionalism. For some, this may be adhering to a formal dress code that makes you feel prepared and capable. For others, it could involve creating detailed lesson plans that provide a sense of control and readiness. Perhaps it is the satisfaction of hearing a pupil say, "Thank you, Sir", or seeing their curiosity as they hang on your every word. Do not think it is possible for all pupils to be rapt in your teaching, but the fact you have some pupils doing this is a good sign of your teaching.

Whatever fuels your enthusiasm for teaching, embrace it as a source of strength. Remember that teaching is a career that spans decades, and self-improvement is a natural and ongoing part of the journey.

Embracing subject communities

No teacher has a complete mastery of every aspect of their subject. This is not a weakness but a shared reality among educators. Whether it is teaching rivers in Geography for the first time or exploring pop art in art, gaps in knowledge are opportunities for growth.

Subject communities provide invaluable support for addressing these challenges. These may exist within your multi-academy trust (MAT), your local area or through national subject-specific organisations. Regular gatherings, both online and in person, offer practical advice, resources and the chance to connect with others who may have faced similar challenges.

Your subject lead should ensure your department is connected to the relevant national body for your subject. These organisations often provide continuing professional development (CPD) opportunities that are tailored to your needs. By engaging with these communities, you gain not only knowledge but also the reassurance that you are part of a collective of professionals who share your experiences.

Being an active member of a subject community is a powerful example of resilience and growth. It allows you to draw on the collective expertise of others, share your own insights, and continue developing in your role. By focusing on your strengths, seeking out support and embracing opportunities for professional growth, you will not only enhance your confidence but also solidify your place as a valued and effective teacher within your school and MAT and further enhance the trust and autonomy senior leaders will place in you.

Developing your career

This section of the chapter will help to retain teachers in the teaching profession through personal ownership of individual development. It will set out how teachers can take responsibility for their own career through strategic planning and self-CPD. It will look at the level of medium and long-term planning needed within teaching. The section will go on to set out how to implement steps to be taken in career development with guidance on how to identify goals ensuring a smooth and meaningful personalised career. The section is frank and realistic in setting out the need to consider a second career as an older teacher due to the nature of teaching and the impact of long-term stress. It will give examples and scenarios of strategies such as wording of difficult emails, taking control of the agenda of meetings, being assertive and confident in approaching line managers, heads of departments and other school leaders. The handling of unsupportive line managers and budget constraints, as well as whole school generic CPD, will be explored with scenarios, examples and guidelines.

Develop yourself rather than wait for others to develop you

One of the key strategies we emphasise in this book is about being earning your own autonomy through strategic planning and self-directed CPD. Rather than waiting for development opportunities to come to you, feel encouraged to proactively map out your career path, setting both immediate and long-term goals. Although your school will have a CPD programme, the CPD programme will, quite naturally, be tightly tailored to outcomes which are good for the school rather than for individual teachers. This is what CPD leads learn in their NPQLTD – connect all CPD to school-centred outcomes. You should reflect on *your* needs, identifying personal interests, strengths and areas for growth, and then seeking out CPD activities that align with these goals. Be prepared to pay small amounts of money to attend online training, which is wholly in your own interest. Whilst school leaders may be quick to deny requests from staff for external CPD, if you pay for it yourself then they cannot stall you in your ambitions to develop yourself in a direction of your own choosing. Self-directed CPD enables you to tailor your learning and development to your unique aspirations, creating a career trajectory that reflects your ambitions and values. Medium- and long-term planning is also crucial; by setting clear career objectives for the future, you will cultivate a more fulfilling and sustainable professional journey.

Another significant element is aligning your career goals with personal values and interests. You should reflect on what you find most meaningful about your teaching, whether it is supporting pupils through their Personal and Social Education, your love for a particular subject, or whether it is fostering an inclusive classroom environment that gets you passionate. By aligning your professional pursuits with these values, you can ensure that their work remains rewarding and personally significant, reducing the risk of burnout. It is all very well working all the hours in pursuit of a school outcome, but if it is not developing you in an area which you are passionate about at the same time then it will be an ineffective way to grow you as a teacher and your career.

The future is always uncertain

One of the things we have said in this book is that schools and trust change, often rapidly. This is because of a high turnover in school leadership teams and also because the context of a school itself can rapidly change in terms of its intake and cohorts. You should always think about what the future holds for you. You may need to consider being able to switch in and out of teaching temporarily or permanently if that is what your career or life circumstances require. Preparing for such eventualities means that you will have a greater sense of future security as you go through your teaching career. You will be well poised to exploit sudden opportunities, and you will also be in a good place should circumstances dictate. You cannot know what the future holds. You may need to move suddenly to take care of a close relative, to follow your partner's career trajectory, to enable your child to attend a specific school – there are many reasons you may need to move teaching jobs or leave teaching at short notice. You should always be looking to develop your qualifications and experiences beyond just being a teacher in order to prepare for such eventualities. For example, it is all very well doing National Professional Qualifications (NPQs), but these qualifications are very school-specific and, in qualification terms, have little value or equivalency. For example, if you studied for a master's in Science, this is an internationally recognised qualification which also qualifies you for further training opportunities such as becoming a qualified Educational Psychologist. Masters and PhDs are recognised in all professions and can ensure you can switch to alternative careers more readily than if you only hold a bachelor's degree, qualified teacher status and an NPQ.

As a teacher, you often face the challenge of composing sensitive or complex emails or undertaking tricky telephone calls or leading sensitive meetings. It takes seriously good communication skills to convey clarity and professionalism in all of these contexts. If you ask any senior leader in education or other industries, they will cite these communication skills as essential to the necessary skill set needed to be successful in their industry. You should look to develop confidence in communication in all of these areas and use that confidence when you are communicating with school leaders. This will help you build positive relationships with your line managers and other senior leaders who will take notice of your professional communication skills. The next time they think of someone for an opportunity or a promotion they will think back to those that impressed them during their interactions, and you want your name to be front and centre of that list!

Navigating toxic line managers

Another aspect of career management involves navigating unsupportive line managers, and senior leaders (whether within the school or from the trust). The general rule of thumb when you run into a toxic leader is to obtain a position elsewhere as soon as you can without suffering any toxic fallout. However, there are many stories of poor references being withheld or opportunities to take up new roles dashed on the foundation of poor working relationships between teachers and senior leaders. If you find yourself needing to extricate yourself from a school, desist from firing off angry or 'hot' emails to senior leaders in the school or trust. Keep a low profile and look professional and committed at all times. If you find yourself on the receiving end of a malicious improvement plan or similar, then involve your union at the earliest opportunity. They can agree to a neutral reference and other outcomes if it is needed. It is a sad thing to say about the system in England, but there is no denying that these things do happen, and you need to be alert to whether your new role is toxic or if a toxic person is elevated or hired into a position of power over you.

The reality of most schools in England is that they have a strong whole-school generic CPD offer for you as a means for individual and collective growth. Your participation in such school-wide professional development initiatives not only enhances your knowledge and skills but also helps foster a supportive and collaborative school or trust environment across the community of practice. Schools find that such CPD activities help teachers like you stay connected with broader educational trends and enable you all to share your insights with your colleagues.

By actively planning your career, aligning your personal and professional goals with your foundational values, and adopting strategic workplace actions, you can empower yourself to achieve long-term job satisfaction, promotions (if that is something you desire) and build resilience within the teaching profession.

Resignations to start work in September

This section provides essential guidance for teachers in England on applying for jobs, understanding resignation deadlines, and navigating employment-related decisions. It aligns with the principles outlined in the Burgundy Book, ensuring compliance with standard practices. You can read this guidance by googling the term 'burgundy book'. The Burgundy Book is a handbook setting out the conditions of service for schoolteachers in England and Wales. Its main provisions relate to notice periods, sick leave and pay and maternity leave and pay. Teachers must give 2 months' notice at all times, except for the final term in which the notice is 3 months. To start on 1 September you will need to resign by 31 May.

This is typically the time when many teachers resign so there will be plenty of jobs options. Unlike those who resign in October or December, resigning between Easter and 31 May allows you to seek new employment from a much wider range of opportunities. Furthermore, you will start your new job with many new teachers so there will be many to support joining your new setting. The number of new starters in September is usually higher, so you will be less lonely with more colleagues in the onboarding process.

April 10 days

Introduction

As exam season approaches, April focuses on effective revision strategies and evaluating sequences of learning. This chapter provides guidance on planning meaningful revision sessions, using evidence-informed practice to ensure pupils are well-prepared for their exams. It also emphasises the importance of reflecting on teaching methods and adapting centralised planning to better meet the needs of your pupils.

Revision strategies

This section of the chapter will support the planning of revision. The pre-exam months are often dominated with centralised planning, which is not always suitable for the needs of specific classes. Some schools may not be applying retrieval practice correctly and the evidence behind study techniques and how they can be applied to revision will be set out in this section.

Delivering effective GCSE revision lessons

GCSE revision is an integral part of the school calendar, particularly in the months of March and April, as preparations intensify before the May exams. The sheer range of revision strategies available can feel overwhelming, but with thoughtful planning and a focus on meaningful methods, you can ensure high-quality revision takes place and revision that genuinely supports your pupils.

Building confidence through understanding

A deep understanding of the exam board's requirements is the cornerstone of effective revision planning. Pupils will sense the confidence in your words and body language as you articulate a clear grasp of the exam criteria. This confidence will inspire trust in your ability to guide them through the process.

DOI: 10.4324/9781032712178-9

To achieve this clarity, you should study exam board reports from the past two or three years, analyse previous exam papers, and identify recurring themes or question types. Many exam boards offer free or online training sessions that can help deepen your understanding. If you have proficiency in IT, creating a spreadsheet to track the frequency and focus of questions can be invaluable. This will allow you to determine exactly what needs attention and what can be deprioritised. If a poem has been used one year, it is unlikely to feature the next. You would still teach the poem, but not as one which might feature. Such nuance is worth extra marks for your particular pupils.

It is essential to avoid appearing uncertain during this critical period, as it may undermine your professionalism and the pupils' confidence in your guidance. Taking the time to prepare thoroughly will ensure you can deliver clear and focused revision lessons.

Knowing your pupils

To deliver meaningful revision, it is vital to have a strong understanding of the pupils in your class. This goes beyond academic ability and includes recognising the nuances of their personalities, motivations and interests. Knowing how to keep each pupil engaged can make a significant difference in their revision outcomes.

For instance, understanding that a pupil has a keen interest in football or music can help you tailor examples or discussion points to capture their attention. By building a positive relationship, you can avoid becoming another voice of negativity in their lives and instead serve as a source of encouragement and support. This guidance may involve personalised advice on tackling specific question types, improving time management, or refining their use of key terminology. In Mathematics, for example, it could mean assessing each pupil's ability to handle one-mark, two-mark, or eight-mark questions and using this knowledge to plan targeted revision strategies.

Effective use of exam practice

Exam practice is an essential component of any revision plan. Practice questions are widely available online, and departments can collaborate to create tailored practice papers that suit the needs of your pupils. Ideally, pupils should have completed several practice papers by this stage, as well as multiple attempts at similar question styles.

Encourage pupils to reflect on their performance in these tasks, identifying their strengths and areas for improvement. This reflection can guide your planning, ensuring that revision sessions address gaps in knowledge and reinforce key skills.

Creative and adaptive revision strategies

Revision does not have to follow a one-size-fits-all approach. Incorporating creative and innovative methods can help maintain pupils' engagement and make the process more enjoyable. Techniques such as group discussions, interactive quizzes, or using visual aids can provide variety and stimulate interest. If you are a new member of staff and are less familiar with your Year 11 cohort, do not hesitate to draw on the expertise of colleagues who have stronger relationships with the pupils. Adopting established strategies that pupils are already accustomed to is not a sign of weakness but rather a pragmatic approach to ensuring their success.

Empowering pupils for self-study

Ultimately, empowering pupils to take ownership of their revision is one of the most effective ways to ensure their success. Equip them with tools and techniques that promote independent learning, such as retrieval practice, effective summarising, mind-mapping or using revision apps. Provide clear guidance on how to use their time effectively and how to approach self-assessment. Encourage pupils to view revision as a collaborative effort between teacher and pupil. With the right preparation, motivation and strategies in place, your pupils can enter the exam period with confidence in their abilities and the tools they need to succeed.

Evaluating sequences of learning and pedagogical practice

This section of the chapter will set out ways for teachers to support their reflection and evolution as teachers as they come to the end of centralised plans for teaching GCSE and A levels. It will ensure that teachers are aware that the centralised planning of teaching and subsequent delivery is always followed by some reflection to ensure it is relevant and appropriate. The section will revisit the need for teachers to be evidence-informed so that they are well-positioned to influence centralised planning and policy with evidence from valued academic sources. This section of the chapter will give several practical ways to structure critical thinking so that teachers can produce effective reflections leading to adaptations to centralised planning.

What to do when you complete teaching a unit

As you get to the end of your centralised plans for teaching GCSE and A levels, you now have a fantastic opportunity – and a bit of a challenge – to tweak your teaching methods to better fit your pupils and classrooms. All the way through your training, you will have been encouraged to be reflective and review how well you matched your teaching to your pupils. And that sums up possibly the weakest aspects of centralised planning: it is all very well planning a scintillating sequence of learning, but if the pupils did not learn well or did not do well in their assessments (and they are two different things) then you need to reflect on why. For example, you might have embedded retrieval practice throughout the sequence of learning and your pupils retrieved very well from your cues, but when it came to the real assessment, they struggled to transfer the cued learning to the real examinations. That is a very modern error in which, instead of getting the pupils to retrieve from multiple unknown cues to retrieve as part of an entangled unknown assessment, you relied on the pre-cued retrieval that was contained within the centralised planning. Sometimes, for teachers, the only way they realise this is when their pupils struggle with an assessment and they have to reflect on why this happened and what they could have done differently. The reality is often that all centralised planning will need to be adapted to the pupils in the class in front of you.

The reflection phase of teaching

Teaching is a dynamic cycle: centralised planning, teaching and then reflective evaluation as you get to the end of the unit or section that you have been teaching. This reflection phase isn't just an afterthought; it is a crucial chance for you to see how well the prescribed content and methods match your classroom realities. For instance, after a unit on Shakespeare, you might reflect on how well your pupils understood and recalled the themes and quotations to support the themes in their inference and analytical work. By understanding this cycle, you can use reflection intentionally, turning it into a tool for insights that can affect your future planned teaching. You cannot reflect on the teaching in an isolated context. Your pupils are unique and you yourself are unique. Did you make assumptions about the learning that affected how you taught or how your pupils learned? For example, some teachers are unaware of the difference between recognition and recall when beginning the process of embedding strong recall in lessons. These teachers could well have been the authors of your centralised planning. Instead of starting with multiple choice questions or matching exercises before moving to un-cued recall and then considering the need for pupils to transfer their learning to novel contexts, they might have gone straight into writing lists of recall questions and putting them into all the lessons, perhaps at the start of every planned lesson.

One of the things this book is consistent on is on you, as a teacher being assertive and knowledgeable about how teaching works rather than just accepting that which is given to you. A teacher who knows that centralised resources are not founded on good ideas about teaching but is told to deliver them regardless will not only feel disempowered, but also start to look elsewhere for employment as a teacher. A teacher who uses evidence and wider reading to help them propose meaningful changes to centralised planning and resources is one that is going to be more likely to be listened to and find their proposals accepted. All teachers must reflect on the fact that their way of doing things is not the only way to teach, and further, their understanding of how learning happens may well become dated or proven to be faddish or a myth. All teachers must be open to critical reflection and work collaboratively to try and ensure their planning, resources and outcomes are ahead of the curve, not beholden to outdated ideas.

Grounding reflection in evidence

For reflection to drive meaningful changes, it needs to be based on evidence. You should use credible sources like peer-reviewed research, subject-specific pedagogy and professional development materials. For example, if you notice that your pupils struggle with algebra, you might look into subject-specific research on effective algebra teaching strategies. However, if that does not work, then perhaps it is your understanding of non-subject-specific pedagogies or ideas about how pupils learn that is holding back the learning of your pupils. By grounding your reflections in evidence, you can confidently suggest adaptations to your department or the MAT central planning team that improve pupil outcomes and show that your contributions to the planning process should be respected.

Using reflective frameworks

Structured reflective frameworks can help you navigate critical thinking. Tools like Clayton's DEAL model (Describe, Examine, Assess, Learn) offer a systematic approach, whereas other tools such as Gibbs' Reflective Cycle and Kolb's Experiential Learning Cycle are very popular with teachers in England.

Clayton's DEAL model

Calyton's DEAL model (Describe, Examine, Assess and Learn), provides you with a framework for your reflection. In the "describe" phase, you recount your experiences, focusing on what happened, who was involved, where and when the events took place and why they occurred. This could, for example, be a lesson where learning was poor, or the centralised planning and resources left you feeling underprepared or the resources were not a good fit for your personal class of pupils. This detailed description then sets the stage for deeper analysis.

During the "examine" phase, you critically analyse the experience from dual perspectives, considering: your own reactions as well as the reactions of your pupils. You then consider the overall effectiveness of your actions during your teaching. This phase is crucial for identifying underlying patterns and gaining a deeper understanding of the experience. How did you react when pupils seemed disaffected or to find they could not retrieve learning effectively? Or they display visible difficulties maintaining attention to the resources? You don't just examine before and after the lesson but consider during the lesson.

The "assess" phase of Clayton's DEAL model involves evaluating the learning that took place, identifying what was learned, how it was learned, and why it was important that your pupils learned it. You should reflect on how you know that your pupils learned it and not forget that we cannot assess within a lesson whether a pupil has learned it because they could immediately forget it. We want the learning to be sticky and therefore they recall it later, and further, transfer it to novel tasks or problems.

Finally, in the "learn" phase, you capture your insights from the reflection cycle and plan how to apply this knowledge to future teaching scenarios or even just to make edits to centralised planning or resources if that is what you think is needed. It might be that you edit the resources and planning for your own personal use as it is quite normal for teachers to have nuanced versions of centralised planning and resources.

Gibbs' reflective cycle

Gibbs' Reflective Cycle is another valuable tool for you and one that might be familiar if you undertook a PGCE into teacher education in England. It consists of six stages: description, feelings, evaluation, analysis, conclusion and action plan. In the "description" stage, you provide a detailed account of the experience, similar to the "describe" phase in the DEAL model. The "feelings" stage involves exploring your emotional responses to the experience, which can offer important insights into personal biases and emotional triggers. This is quite a normal thing in teaching – we, as teachers, react to pupils and their learning experiences in an emotional way, and this can give us personal insights into the lens through which we look at teaching. The "evaluation" stage requires you to assess what was, in your personal opinion, good and bad about the experience, providing a balanced view of the events. A key thing is to not consider a lesson all bad – there will always be positives, and some pupils will have learned well even if not all pupils did. During the "analysis" stage, you delve deeper into understanding why things happened the way they did, considering both internal and external factors. The "conclusion" stage involves summarising what has been learned from the experience, and the "action plan" stage focuses on how to apply these lessons to future teaching practices, ensuring that the reflection leads to change in your approach to teaching. Teachers who train in England often learn this cycle and use it to help them elevate their teaching to a higher standard.

Kolb's Experiential Learning Cycle

Kolb's Experiential Learning Cycle is another reflective model commonly studied and used by teachers who train in England. It emphasises learning through experience and reflection and comprises four stages: concrete experience, reflective observation, abstract conceptualisation and active experimentation.

In the "concrete experience" stage, you engage in a specific teaching activity or encounter a particular event. This has been developed by some to become the "unseen" observation lesson. In other words, you undertake Kolb's experiential learning cycle in tandem with a mentor who does not observe the lesson. Rather you reflect on the lesson afterwards with the mentor. Thus, the next stage is the 'reflective observation' stage, which involves stepping back and reflecting on the experience, considering what happened and why – with or without a mentor, as explained. During the "abstract conceptualisation" stage, you develop theories or concepts based on your reflections, linking your experiences to broader educational principles and theories. Finally, in the "active experimentation" stage, you apply your new insights to future teaching situations, testing out new strategies and approaches in your classroom, implementing then and undertaking further cycles of the reflective cycle. You might also use these thoughts to influence your editing of centralised planning and resources so that others can benefit from your reflection.

Integrating reflection models in your teaching practice

By integrating the DEAL model, Gibbs' Reflective Cycle or Kolb's Experiential Learning Cycle into your reflective practice, you can gain a comprehensive understanding of your experiences, identify areas for improvement in centralised planning and resources, and develop effective strategies for enhancing your teaching. Each model offers unique strengths: the DEAL model's structured approach ensures thorough analysis and practical application, Gibbs' Reflective Cycle emphasises emotional awareness and balanced evaluation, and Kolb's cycle highlights the importance of linking theory to practice. Together, these models provide a robust framework for reflection, empowering you to continuously evolve and excel in your profession. What is important is that you draw from all the models to deliver key outcomes: structured reflection, an awareness of the affective domain and how it influences your teaching and lastly knowledge of evidence and theory which you can bring in to strengthen your future teaching, planning and design of resources.

Encouraging collaborative reflection

As mentioned in the last section, with the idea of an unseen observation, reflection doesn't have to be a solo activity. Engaging in peer-to-peer collaboration and dialogue with your teaching colleagues or leaders brings fresh perspectives, challenges assumptions and uncovers blind spots. For example, we all know that when we are struggling with a challenging class, then a chat with a colleague leads us to try new strategies for managing classroom behaviour. This is especially valuable for you if you are an early career teacher who can benefit from the mentorship of more experienced peers. However, no matter how experienced a teacher is, they can always learn from collaborative work and co-reflection. Having a critical friend is a bedrock in understanding how teaching and learning work in secondary schools in England.

Reflection as a lever for progress

Evaluating your sequences of learning, resources (whether they are booklets or slides) and teaching practices is a key part of a teacher's professional development. Through evidence-based reflection, structured frameworks and collaborative dialogue, you can effectively adapt centralised planning to better serve your pupils and colleagues. In doing so, you play an assertive, autonomous and crucial role in shaping the educational systems in your department to ensure that they are flexible, responsive and ready for the future.

May 20 days

Introduction

May is a time for assertive professionalism and managing pre-exam conversations with parents. This chapter offers advice on handling difficult conversations with parents, addressing unconscious bias and maintaining professionalism in challenging situations. It provides practical examples and strategies to help you navigate these situations with confidence and assertiveness.

Assertive professionalism

In this section of the chapter, teachers will be given scenarios and advice on how to deal with awkward or confrontational conversations, interactions or situations with pupils or parents during the start of exam season. The notions of assertive professionalism, such as being polite and professional yet not being seen to be too passive and not being able to maintain one's self-respect, will be set out. Some examples of how to confront a toxic or confrontational colleague will be explored. In addition, there will be a recognition of the unconscious bias that teachers can face from pupils, staff and parents within the school community alongside some statutory instruction on how to deal with discrimination.

Managing pre-exam conversations with parents

Pre-exam season often brings an increased need for communication with parents. Some parents may be highly supportive and engaged in their child's education, while others may be less supportive or hold unrealistic expectations. As teachers, we must navigate these conversations with sensitivity, professionalism and preparation.

If a pupil has incomplete work or has not been performing to their potential, it is essential to have a record of their lack of engagement and the interventions that have been attempted. Evidence-based conversations are a hallmark of professionalism in teaching. Prepare data from assessments, attendance records, examples of classwork and behavioural reports, including any sanctions or rewards. These records will provide a solid foundation for discussing a pupil's progress or areas for improvement with their parents, especially if they request a meeting and you feel the request is to discuss reasons why their child is not doing so well with a subtext that it could be your fault rather than the child.

Handling difficult conversations

In instances where parents may become aggressive or defensive, it is vital to remain calm and professional. Having a loose script or key phrases prepared can help maintain focus and avoid escalation. For example:

- **Negative realities:**
    - "Observations in class have shown that your child has occasionally been uncooperative, and this has impacted their learning."
    - "Your child often becomes distracted when working in groups, which affects their focus and outcomes."
    - "We have offered several support opportunities, such as revision classes and after-school sessions, but attendance has been inconsistent."
    - "Their work has not met the standard expected of a pupil with their potential."

- **Positive praise:**
    - "Your child has demonstrated the potential to achieve their expected grade through strong work and exams."
    - "To reach their potential, your child needs to focus on improving specific areas, such as [list specific skills or behaviours]."
    - "We have seen steady improvement in their attainment from X to Y, which is encouraging."

Toxic colleagues and professional boundaries

Like all professions, schools are not immune to interpersonal challenges. Working closely with colleagues can sometimes lead to tensions. To maintain a positive working environment and protect your own well-being, consider the following strategies:

- **Set clear boundaries:** ensure interactions are rooted in professionalism. While collaboration is essential, there is no obligation to socialise beyond what is required.

- **Use official communication channels:** communicate key information through emails, ensuring your tone remains polite and focused on the matter at hand. Whatever you do, refrain from writing emotive long and combative emails. It really will not help.

- **Find safe spaces:** identify a positive environment where you can take breaks, whether that is the staffroom, your classroom or another supportive area within the school.

Assertiveness will vary depending on individual confidence and comfort with confrontation. Consider the following examples:

- **Teacher A:** if timetabled to teach yet another challenging group, you may prefer to email your head of department, providing two or three well-reasoned points about why a change might be necessary. Avoid presenting a long list of grievances, as this could be seen as excessive complaining.

- **Teacher B:** if you are asked to help with sports day but are not comfortable in such roles, communicate your preferences politely to the Physical Education (PE) department and follow up with an email if necessary. This can prevent future misunderstandings about your willingness to take on similar tasks.

- **Teacher C:** if you disagree with feedback from a lesson observation, approach the matter professionally. Acknowledge any valid criticisms, but be prepared to defend your practice where appropriate, particularly if you feel your adaptive teaching strategies have been misjudged. Again and again, in this book, we have said – autonomy is earned, and it needs to be earned through evidence-informed knowledge and opinions.

Addressing unconscious bias

Unconscious bias can subtly permeate even the most inclusive of school environments, influencing interactions between teachers, pupils and colleagues. As professional teachers, recognising and addressing these biases is crucial to our ability to create a fair and inclusive culture within the school. Bias may emerge in assumptions about teachers' abilities, interests or perspectives based on factors such as gender, ethnicity, socioeconomic background or subject specialism.

Recognising bias

Teachers may encounter bias in several forms:

- **Stereotyping based on gender or role:** for example, assumptions about a teacher's interests or capabilities linked to their subject area or gender.

- **Judgements tied to ethnicity or background:** teachers may face assumptions about their values, approach to teaching, or expectations based on their cultural or socioeconomic background.

- **Professional pigeonholing:** teachers who demonstrate skill or knowledge in one area may find themselves overlooked for opportunities in others due to preconceived ideas about their strengths.

These biases, often unintentional, can undermine professional relationships, career progression and self-confidence.

Responding assertively

Challenging unconscious bias in secondary schools requires both assertiveness and diplomacy. It is essential to address issues in a way that promotes understanding while safeguarding your professional relationships and position. It is very easy to respond in a way which leads to you having to leave the school, and, really, you want to avoid that if it is a good school. Bias will exist; it is a human condition. We can challenge it without confrontation. Here are strategies to consider:

1. **Acknowledge the bias calmly:** if you feel a fellow teacher's comment or assumption reflects bias, address it politely but directly. For instance, you might say, "I understand why you might think that, but I approach things a little differently," before clarifying your perspective or approach.

2. **Seek constructive dialogue:** if a pattern of bias emerges, consider initiating a conversation with the relevant colleague or manager. Frame your concerns in a solution-focused manner, such as, "I have noticed people seem to make this assumption about me. How can I make them feel differently?"

3. **Document your experiences:** keeping a professional record of any incidents or patterns of bias can provide clarity and support if further action becomes necessary. It is a sad thing to say, but standard union advice in school is to keep a clear log and evidence trail of anything untoward. You never know when you might need it.

4. **Use MAT or school HR policies:** many MATs or schools have diversity and inclusion policies or staff well-being frameworks as part of their HR setup. Familiarising yourself with these policies can provide a supportive structure for raising concerns or suggesting improvements, and ensure you follow policy. Not following policy will leave you vulnerable and in a position where those biased against you will be in a stronger position.

Parents' evenings (from January to May)

This section will explore the best ways to maximise interactions with the parents of pupils whether it is traditional or online. It will set out how online parents' evenings work as some teachers may not have had experience of these. It will set out how each year group requires at least one parent evening, meaning there may be as many as six per academic year. This section will set out the objective of building an honest and productive relationship with parents with example scenarios and strategies to present to parents on improving the outcomes of their children. There will be a focus on dealing with parents of challenging children who are supportive, as well as challenging parents whether their children are challenging or not.

Parents' evenings, whether face-to-face or online, are essential for building strong partnerships between schools and families. These events provide a platform to discuss pupils' progress, address concerns and encourage collaboration to ensure pupils go through school feeling safe and supported. While the purpose remains the same across both formats, the delivery differs, requiring teachers to adapt their approach to maximise the effectiveness of these interactions.

Each year group typically has at least one parents' evening annually, creating several opportunities to engage with families. These meetings aim to strengthen trust, encourage collaboration and ensure transparency between you and the parents or carers of the pupils you teach. For you, the goal is to create honest and productive relationships with parents while maintaining professionalism and focus. A good relationship with parents is worth its weight in gold for maximising behaviour, attitude and outcomes.

Traditional and online formats

Face-to-face meetings allow for personal interaction, offering the chance to read non-verbal cues and engage in spontaneous discussions. However, time management can be a challenge in busy schools. You only need one parent to be late and the whole system can rapidly descend into chaos. If that happens, be prepared to problem solve. If a parent does not turn up and you see a later appointment waiting for another teacher, jump them into the earlier slot so that you have some flexibility if the missing parents show up late.

Online meetings provide a more structured environment, with automated time slots that end promptly – this has proved popular for teachers, but less so for parents who would like to continue talking! This system eliminates long queues but introduces the risk of technical difficulties. Teachers must be concise and prepared for interruptions, with plans for follow-up where necessary. Both formats require professionalism, empathy and clear communication to ensure success.

Building honest and productive relationships

Effective communication is the foundation of a successful parents' evening. Conversations should start with strengths to build rapport and then address areas for improvement in a constructive manner. For example, a teacher might say, "Emma's participation in group discussions has been excellent this term, though I have noticed she sometimes struggles with completing her classwork in the designated amount of time. Perhaps we can discuss strategies to support her with her extended writing?"

Engaging parents as partners in their child's education is crucial. Asking open-ended questions about the pupil's experiences at home fosters collaboration and demonstrates respect for the parent's insights. Difficult conversations, such as those involving poor behaviour or low performance, require calm professionalism and a focus on solutions. Teachers can frame these discussions around shared goals, such as "Let us work together to ensure Jake stays on track. A behaviour plan could help us address the disruptions we are seeing in class." Parents do get that a structured behaviour plan can work well for their children and ensure they have an opportunity to show that they can work hard.

Adapting to year groups

Parents' evenings vary in tone and focus depending on the year group. For Year 7, the emphasis is on transition and integration, discussing how pupils are settling socially and academically. In Year 8, the conversation might shift to academic attitude and emerging strengths or challenges. By Year 9, the focus often turns to General Certificate in Secondary Education (GCSE) options and ensuring pupils are prepared for their next steps.

For Year 10 and Year 11, the tone becomes more serious as the discussion centres on performance in key subjects, time management and preparation for exams. Teachers may also address issues like anxiety or burnout, offering strategies to maintain balance during these critical years.

Effective time management

Time management is vital, especially when juggling multiple appointments. Teachers should prepare thoroughly by organising pupil data and pre-filling essential notes. During the meeting, staying concise and focused helps ensure that every parent feels heard within the allocated time.

After the meeting, follow-up is essential to demonstrate commitment. Whether through phone calls, emails, or additional meetings, timely action reassures parents and strengthens the partnership. Parents' evenings are invaluable opportunities to work collaboratively with families for the benefit of pupils. Whether conducted in person or online, these interactions require preparation, adaptability and clear communication. See them as helpful rather than intrusions on your free evening time. Well managed, they can save you time and energy over the year.

Last day for resignations

This section provides essential guidance for teachers in England on applying for jobs, understanding resignation deadlines and navigating employment-related decisions. It aligns with the principles outlined in the Burgundy Book, ensuring compliance with standard practices. You can read this guidance by googling the term "burgundy book." The burgundy book is a handbook setting out the conditions of service for schoolteachers in England and Wales. Its main provisions relate to notice periods, sick leave and pay and maternity leave and pay. Teachers must give two months' notice at all times, except for the final term in which the notice is three months.

For a teacher to leave their current post at the end of the summer term and start a new position in September, the final resignation date is 31 May. This means you must provide written notice by 31 May to ensure your resignation aligns with the notice periods required under the Burgundy Book.

June 15 days

Introduction

June is a month of extracurricular activities and gained time. This chapter highlights the importance of encouraging lifelong healthy habits in your pupils through physical activity and other extracurricular opportunities. It also discusses how to use gained time productively, whether through professional development, updating resources, or preparing for the new academic year. The goal is to make the most of this time to enhance both personal and professional growth.

Extracurricular activities

This section focuses on the way secondary schools in England have a higher range of extracurricular activities due to the inclement weather. The section will set out how, at this time of year, pupils undertake an extended range of activities such as athletics, and this is a good time to cultivate lifelong habits around physical activity. It will explore how the provision of such extracurricular activities is not always related to a subject teacher's actual subject and that many teachers offer extracurricular activities related to their interests rather than simply their subject. It will list examples such as History teachers taking cricket net practice or English teachers running school football teams.

Extracurricular activities in secondary schools

This section explores the wide range of extracurricular activities typically offered in English secondary schools and the role that teachers play in facilitating them. Secondary schools often offer a diverse range of activities, including sports, music, drama, academic opportunities and more. These activities can be an important complement to the formal curriculum, supporting pupils' social and emotional growth, as well as their academic development. Do not think such activities are the preserve of independent and privately funded schools.

If anything, extracurricular activities are even more important in schools that serve deprived communities where access to such activities may be extremely limited.

The purpose of these activities is to help develop within your pupils a range of things, not least, the transferable habitus that will stay with them for life. The pupil who learns to play an instrument in an ensemble learns how to focus independently, how to collaborate and how to perform under pressure. These are all critical attributes which will stand them well in any future scenario – and thus become part of their habitus.

Encouraging lifelong habits

As a teacher, you can play a key role in encouraging your pupils to participate in extracurricular activities. Such participation is beneficial not only for pupils' physical and emotional well-being but also for their personal development. Engaging in sports, drama, performance and other extracurricular activities can help pupils develop valuable skills such as teamwork, leadership, communication and resilience – skills that are transferable to many areas of their current and future lives. Additionally, extracurricular activities provide pupils with opportunities to make new friends and become more connected to their school community. This sense of belonging can help build self-esteem and promote positive mental health, both of which are crucial during the formative years of secondary school. By encouraging participation, you're fostering habits that can last a lifetime.

Subject specialisms and extracurricular activities

While extracurricular activities in secondary schools are often associated with curriculum subjects-drama and performances, English and debates, Maths and the Alan Turing Cryptography Competition, it is not unusual to find that secondary subject teachers frequently lead or assist with activities outside of their subject specialism. For example, you may find a History teacher coaching a school football team, or a Maths teacher leading a chess club. The reason for this is that, just like the world over, people enjoy extracurricular activities beyond the subject they choose to specialise in. In some ways, this is an opportunity for teachers to demonstrate to their pupils that these extracurricular activities are more about being epistemically curious than exploring more learning from a subject. Further, these activities allow teachers to show a human side and share their personal interests with pupils. Experienced teachers will always tell you, once your pupils see you as a human with interests and passions like anyone else, then they begin to form a more human relationship with you. They enter a classroom or a playing field ready to give you updates from a range of extracurricular areas, whether those updates are news from the cricket world, a book they read, something they achieved outside of lesson time, a performance they went to see and so on. They recognise you as someone who has a shared interest and in sharing this with you as a teacher, so they are learning to operate and communicate within the adult world using their extracurricular interests to drive friendships and social groups. This is not to say that as a teacher you are their friend, you are not, you are their teacher. However, by having conversations with you around a shared interest, your pupils learn how people who are interested in that extracurricular area communicate and share information and experiences from that area.

This shift towards interest-based rather than subject-based extracurricular involvement is important to consider as you reflect on your own role within the school. Teachers bring a diverse set of skills and passions to extracurricular programmes, and this diversity enriches pupils' school experiences. You might find that your own hobbies, even those unrelated to your subject specialism, can provide an excellent opportunity for pupil engagement.

The importance of physical activity

As a secondary school teacher, you are likely already aware of the importance of physical activity in promoting your pupils' overall health and well-being. Adolescence is a crucial time for developing lifelong habits, and extracurricular activities such as physical exercise and sports can play an important role in this process. Pupils who grow into physically active adults will have better physical and mental health and reduced long-term health risks.

Currently, around 50% of children meet the UK Chief Medical Officers' guidelines of 60 minutes or more of physical activity per day, a statistic which has remained fairly consistent for a few years. However, the Covid-19 era had a negative impact on younger children who were in nursery to Year 4 during the pandemic. These children, in Years 4–9 (in 2026), show lower positive attitudes towards physical activity and a reduced sense of opportunity. This means you are likely to meet this attitude as you work in the secondary sector and will be part of a national effort to ensure we do not emerge a generation of society with a less positive attitude to physical activity.

It is also important to see the distinction between sports and being physically active. Gyms and fitness classes are full of people who say they dislike participating in sports. Your pupils will be similar. Whilst many do like sports and that participation is good for them, it is not the only way your pupils can be physically active.

By supporting and encouraging participation in physical activities, you help pupils develop habits that can benefit them well beyond their school years. As a teacher, you have the opportunity to create extracurricular environments that motivate and inspire your pupils to take care of their physical and mental health, both in and out of the classroom. And at the same time, you will be staying fit and active as well!

Gained time or re-timetabling

This section addresses a common post-examination issue – once Year 11 and Year 13 classes have completed their examinations, they have the rest of the term off, and you often find your timetable opening up. This gained time offers a rare opportunity to focus on tasks that are difficult to prioritise during busier periods. Schools may approach this differently – some are re-timetable to maximise resources, while others allow teachers more autonomy to use this time productively.

Collaborating with your head of department

A productive starting point is to liaise with your head of department to determine if there are specific tasks or projects requiring attention. This demonstrates professionalism and a proactive attitude. For instance, there may be opportunities to update and organise departmental centralised planning and resources. Sorting through outdated materials and introducing fresh resources can rejuvenate your teaching and provide a chance to implement new ideas that align with your own vision for the department. Remember, autonomy is earned, and by offering to do some of the centralised planning work, you wrest greater control over the environment within which you teach.

Showcasing pupils' work

One valuable use of this time is to refresh display boards with exemplary work from your pupils. There is nothing pupils like more than seeing their work or photos of them in productions or group work on a display board. Displays showcasing high-quality work not only celebrate your pupils' achievements but also set high expectations for others. For example, in art, you might feature Year 10 pieces exploring different artistic techniques, or in History, display Year 8 pupils' detailed timelines of key historical events. These displays should inspire and motivate, creating a positive and aspirational atmosphere within your classroom or departmental display spaces. Remember, even if you are a core subject, you will want your pupils to select your subject for further study.

Enhancing subject knowledge and evidence-informed practice

The additional time can also be dedicated to enhancing subject knowledge and exploring evidence-informed teaching strategies. Engaging with professional literature and resources, such as subject-specific journals or Office for Standards in Education, Children's Services and Skills (OFSTED) subject reports, ensures that your teaching remains current and reflective of best practices. For example, an English teacher might explore research on teaching analytical writing skills, while a Science teacher could investigate new strategies for practicals they are not confident in. These activities not only enhance your expertise but also provide the evidence base needed to support any proposals or changes you wish to implement within your department. You might consider a more formal investigation into your practice, in which case, there is a section in July which shows you how to use a model from the Chartered College of Teaching to achieve this.

Observing colleagues and refining practice

Observing colleagues' lessons is another effective way to utilise this time. Observations provide insight into strategies that may address specific challenges you face, such as improving classroom management or refining lesson transitions. For example, observing how a colleague engages in a challenging Year 8 class might inspire you to approach your own KS3 classes differently.

This is also a good time to recall your annual performance review targets. Whilst they will likely be centred on school-wide metrics, you can still identify areas for professional growth ready to insert into your annual write-up. Schools are increasingly focusing on project-based development over purely results-oriented evaluations. Use this time to complete relevant Continuing Professional Development (CPD), prepare evidence for your targets or start to draft personal goals that align with your broader professional aspirations.

Preparing for the new timetable

If your school decides to roll over the timetable early or introduce new classes, this use of gained time replaces the work you would have done in September. This includes developing seating plans and establishing routines that can help set the tone for a productive and structured environment. For example, they will take time to adjust to you, but at the same time, you need to evaluate them rapidly using a range of assessments for learning strategies so that your teaching is pitched to deliver success.

School trips and out-of-class teaching

This section sets out how in the month of June there is often an escalation in the provision of school trips and out-of-class opportunities for development. It will explain how collapsed timetables work, the health and safety needed to be adhered and offer scenarios that some teachers face when accompanying children during visits where there are greater risks for incidents and issues related to health and safety. The section sets out how being involved in such trips can lead to better relationships within class and more effective long-term learning.

School trips

June is often one of the busiest months in the school year. Not only is the month packed full of exams for your older pupils, but the month of June also sees secondary schools offering a range of school trips and out-of-class activities (sometimes badged 'activity week') that seek to extend learning beyond the traditional classroom setting. These trips, events and experiences are carefully curated to enhance pupils' horizons, their knowledge of the world and to try and foster personal growth. As secondary teachers, we all know that if a pupil has curiosity in something, then that in itself can create a wide range of academic virtues that in themselves lead to positive outcomes in the long term.

A key feature of this busy month is the implementation of what is known as collapsed timetables, where your school pauses regular lessons, freeing up teachers and pupils from their scheduled lessons. This approach means the schools can confidently plan events knowing they have sufficient staffing on hand to help lead and supervise the experiences – whether this is within the school grounds or off-site. For example, an entire week might be dedicated to exploring local historical landmarks, participating in hands-on Science, Technology, Engineering and Maths (STEM) initiatives, or undertaking team-building challenges or the sort that might inspire them to sign up to a Duke of Edinburgh scheme. Such activities not only promote practical, experiential learning but also align with curriculum goals – an important point because parents will want to know their children are experiencing learning opportunities, not just having a fun day out at a theme park.

Ensuring safety and success

The success of school trips and events depends on meticulous planning, with safety as the foremost priority. All teachers involved in trip and event planning must adhere to stringent guidelines, conduct thorough risk assessments and ensure appropriate supervision ratios. Your school will have specific paperwork and expectations and there will be a member of staff who is responsible for overseeing the planning of events and signing off your health and safety planning. Do not be surprised or upset if your first drafts are returned to you for further improvement. Those experienced in the planning of trips and events will know where things can go wrong and will be helpful to you in planning for such eventualities. For example, a trip to a historical site might require assessing how to ensure that pupils can visit toilet facilities that are also frequented by members of the public in a safe and secure manner.

Different types of trips present unique challenges. A visit to a museum or an art gallery may require monitoring pupils in interactive spaces and ensuring they learn about expected conduct and behaviour around exhibits. Meanwhile, a Geography field trip to a coastal area demands more robust contingency planning, such as monitoring weather conditions and establishing safety protocols for water-based risks. In every scenario, careful preparation ensures pupils can explore safely while gaining valuable insights.

Strengthening relationships and enriching learning

Beyond academics, school trips provide an excellent opportunity to strengthen relationships between pupils and teachers. Experiencing activities in a more relaxed, informal environment fosters trust and camaraderie. Whether it's sharing a meal during a picnic or helping a pupil overcome a hiking challenge, these moments contribute to stronger classroom dynamics and a more supportive learning environment.

Moreover, these experiences bring the curriculum to life. A History lesson on the Industrial Revolution becomes much more impactful when pupils visit a preserved factory and see the machinery in action. Similarly, a Biology class is enriched when pupils explore ecosystems firsthand at a local wetland. By connecting theoretical knowledge to real-world contexts, these experiences deepen understanding and make learning more vivid and enduring.

Broadening the scope of education

The focus on school trips and out-of-class learning in June highlights how education can transcend traditional classroom walls. With careful preparation and a steadfast commitment to safety, teachers can transform these excursions into eye-opening opportunities that inspire curiosity, foster community and leave lasting memories. These experiences do more than enhance academic understanding – they contribute to holistic pupil development, equipping learners with the tools to thrive both inside and outside the classroom.

July 13 days

Introduction

In July, the focus is on conducting intervention investigations and maintaining wellbeing ahead of the summer break. This chapter explains how to use gained time to carry out evidence-informed investigations into teaching interventions, enhancing future employability. It also emphasises the importance of maintaining your wellbeing, offering practical advice on managing stress and preparing for the new academic year.

Intervention investigation

This section of the chapter sets out how gained time can be used to increase a teacher's future employability by carrying out evidence-informed investigations into interventions and adaptations to pre-existing planning and teaching. The section looks at the Chartered College for Teaching's model and shows how this model can be adapted by a teacher to both enhance teaching within their school and also enable them to evaluate if the Chartered Teacher Status (CTEACH) is for them.

Maximising gained time

In England's education system, "gained time" presents a rather distinctive opportunity. These periods, which emerge when examination classes conclude and the usual teaching load lightens, are all too often relegated to catching up on marking or administrative tasks. Not all schools have gained time; some schools re-timetable to create new classes after the May half term. However, if your school has gained time, then it can serve as a powerful vehicle for professional growth through carefully structured intervention research.

Understanding intervention research in practice

What do we mean by intervention research in the classroom context? At its heart, it is about methodologically scrutinising specific pedagogical approaches or curriculum adaptations to evaluate their efficacy. This is not merely having a go at something new; rather, it is about bringing academic ideas to your everyday teaching. It is important to understand that what you do with your classes cannot be scaled up. You cannot say your intervention works for all pupils in all schools. However, if you introduce a change and your chosen data gathering tools report a positive outcome then you can claim there was a substantive effect on your participants from your intervention.

A structured framework for investigation

The Chartered College of Teaching's model provides an excellent foundation and is one which has been adapted successfully across various school contexts. The investigation cycle encompasses:

1. Focus Identification: pinpointing a specific aspect of practice worthy of investigation
2. Intervention Design: crafting a considered plan for implementing changes
3. Implementation: putting the intervention into practice whilst maintaining detailed records
4. Evidence Collection: gathering both quantitative and qualitative data systematically
5. Analysis and Reflection: evaluating outcomes and considering implications for future practice

Professional recognition and career progression

The alignment between intervention research and the requirements for Chartered Teacher Status (CTeach) is particularly noteworthy. If you find that you enjoy the academic process of investigating interventions and their impact on your pupils, then you might enjoy undertaking the Chartered College's CTeach qualification. Even more, it might whet your appetite for academic study, and you might consider doing a master's or a doctorate. All of those qualifications can be done whilst you are teaching, and you do not have to give up your career to undertake academic work.

The ripple effects of intervention research extend well beyond individual classrooms. When teachers share their findings through INSET sessions or departmental meetings, they contribute to a cascade effect of evidence-based improvement. Whilst your particular work might not be generalisable, it might spark an idea in a colleague who has a similar issue or challenge within their pupils. Remember, senior leaders in schools and MATs are always on the lookout for the next school improvement champion. Whilst we are short of teachers, there is a competitive market for strong senior leaders in the education sector and evidence of systematic professional development can set candidates apart. Intervention research provides concrete examples of initiative, analytical thinking and commitment to improvement. During interviews, you can draw upon specific investigations that demonstrate your capacity for innovation and impact – something that is particularly effective in advancement to middle and senior leadership positions.

Moving forward

To maximise gained time through intervention research:

- Choose investigations that align with both personal interests and school development plans
- Maintain thorough records of your process and findings
- Seek opportunities to share insights with colleagues during CPD sessions
- Consider how your research might contribute to wider educational discourse

By approaching gained time as an opportunity for structured investigation rather than merely administrative catch-up, you can simultaneously enhance your practice, contribute to school improvement and advance your career.

Wellbeing and personal satisfaction

This section looks at a time of year when teachers are very tired, and pupils are often restless for their summer holidays. The section sets out how it can be a period characterised by larger than normal pupil absence, as well as a time when teacher wellbeing can be at its lowest. It goes on to offer a range of scenarios with advice for each one about how to respond to both challenges and opportunities.

Not all pupils look forward to summer

For many pupils, the summer holidays represent a time of excitement and freedom, with activities and family trips to look forward to. However, for others, the prospect of six weeks away from school can be daunting. Pupils who rely on school for structure, social interaction or even regular hot meals may find this transition stressful. Recognising this diversity of experiences can help you understand why some pupils may display variable emotions or challenging behaviour in the final weeks of term.

For example, a Year 7 pupil who frequently acts out in class might be anxious about spending the summer in an unstructured environment at home or being looked after by extended family or even an estranged parent. Understanding this context allows you to approach such situations with empathy, offering support rather than reacting with frustration.

Maintaining your wellbeing

The rewards of teaching are not limited to the summer break, but it is important to arrive at the holidays in a state that allows you to truly enjoy and benefit from them. Some teachers absolutely collapse into their summer break, devoid of energy and health. This means you waste the first ten days of your break simply recovering. You want to arrive to the summer break ready to have a real holiday from teaching. This requires you prioritising your wellbeing during the final term.

- **Dietary adjustments:** Eating lighter meals with more fruits and vegetables and fewer carbohydrates can help maintain energy levels, reducing the lethargy that often accompanies the end of a busy year. Really make an effort to not rely on sugary carbs and convenience food and supercharge your body with high-quality nutrition.

- **Planning for the holidays:** Having something to look forward to – a day trip, a holiday, or simply time to unwind – provides a mental boost and serves as a light at the end of the tunnel. Try and put some plans into place so that as you finish, you have alternative things to do – even if they do not cost anything.

Managing behaviour

Behaviour management at this time of year requires flexibility and perspective. For instance, dealing with a persistently challenging pupil, such as a disruptive Year 8, can feel particularly draining. However, it is essential to remind yourself that such behaviour may not reflect your teaching but rather external factors. Focus on what is within your control and let the school's behaviour management systems address issues wherever possible. Do not let up or be lax – consistency is key to good behaviour, even if the summer holidays are impending.

Adapting to timetable changes

End-of-term activities, such as collapsed timetables, sports days, or activity days, often bring a shift in routines. Pupils may exhibit behaviour that, while inappropriate for a typical classroom, is more acceptable in these informal settings. Embrace this flexibility and use these events as opportunities to build rapport with pupils. If pupils are doing drama activities then laughter and some silliness are part of how they deal with the embarrassment of doing drama. The same is true when they are doing some kind of physical activity. Whilst these things are normal for a subject teacher, if you are helping to supervise an activity outside of your subject area you might see behaviour that you are unused to. Sometimes, it can be an improvement in behaviour that you see. For instance, a Year 9 pupil who has been difficult in your class might excel in a STEM activity or show leadership during a sports day. This is your opportunity to step in, recognising and acknowledging these positive behaviours and significantly improve your relationship with them in the future.

Addressing absences

In England, some parents may choose to take their children out of school early for more affordable holidays. This is against the law, and they can be fined, but it does not stop it from happening. While this can disrupt group activities or planned lessons, it is important to remain adaptable. Discuss any major impacts with your head of department and ensure you are liaising with the relevant school staff who will be monitoring absences. It will not be just you who has missing pupils, all teachers will. This means it will be a whole school issue with a whole school action plan of which you can play a strong part.

Looking ahead

The final weeks of the summer term are not just about managing fatigue and behaviour –they also provide a chance to reflect and prepare for the year ahead. Use this time to consolidate relationships, celebrate achievements and set the stage for a fresh start in September. You might be seeing some of your Year 9 pupils back in September to start their GCSEs, and you can help them get ready for this by talking about the upcoming curriculum and what they can do to help prepare for it. By approaching this pre-summer period with empathy, flexibility and self-care, you can transform the challenges of the summer term into opportunities for growth, connection and renewal – for your pupils and for yourself.

August 2 days

Introduction

Finally, August is all about GCSE and A-level results days as well as preparing for September. This chapter provides guidance on supporting your pupils with their results, managing the clearing process and advising on post-16 and post-18 options. It emphasises the importance of celebrating achievements and providing clear, supportive advice to help pupils navigate their next steps. It also covers how to get your teaching space reading for September – especially if you are starting as a brand new teacher in the school.

GCSE results day

This section sets out how schools approach GCSE results day and manage the release of results for their pupils. It sets out the impact of the GCSEs on pupils in accessing the next stage of their career and education and sets out an array of example paths from apprenticeships to universities that a teacher might speak to a parent and their child about on exam day. The section is factual about the requirements for access to post-16 education and how to best advise children and parents on appeal arrangements and so forth.

GCSE results day: Celebrating and supporting pupils and parents

GCSE results day is the biggest and most serious landmark day in the secondary academic calendar – bigger than A-level results day because all pupils in secondary schools in England will have results on that day. It is filled with excitement, anxiety, the potential of new opportunities and, we have to be honest, for some pupils there will be negative emotions as well. For teachers, it represents a critical point in the school calendar to provide guidance, support and clarity as pupils transition to the next stage of their education or career journey. Your role is to ensure that pupils and their families are well-informed, reassured and empowered to make decisions that align with their aspirations and circumstances.

DOI: 10.4324/9781032712178-13

The significance of GCSEs

GCSE qualifications in England often serve as the gateway to post-16 education and training. Whether your pupils aspire to enter sixth form, enrol in a college, begin an apprenticeship, or move directly into the workforce, their results usually play a significant role in shaping their options. Achieving a Grade 4 or higher in English and Mathematics is typically a minimum requirement for many pathways. Indeed, if they do not achieve those Grade 4s in English and Maths, they will have to continue studying them and retake them as part of the requirements for post-16 study. However, some vocational courses or apprenticeships may offer some limited flexibility, providing tailored support for pupils needing to retake key subjects. With around 30% not passing their GCSE English and Mathematics in England, depending on your school, you could find yourself having to explain this to those worried they will not be able to access post-16 training or apprenticeships.

Providing guidance on pathways

On results day, it is vital for you to be equipped with a broad understanding of the pathways available to pupils. Here are some helpful guidelines you can use to advise your pupils and their parents:

- **Sixth Form and A levels:** many of your pupils will aim to continue their studies in either your school or another school (quite a few schools are only 11–16), sixth form college or further education college by pursuing A levels or even the International Baccalaureate. You can help parents and pupils consider subject choices that align with career aspirations, such as understanding what A levels to select for specific degrees. For example, parents might have the misconception that only Biology, Chemistry and Mathematics are suitable for a future in medicine. The reality is as follows:

    a. Chemistry: almost all medical courses require Chemistry at A level.

    b. Biology: many medical courses also require Biology.

    c. Mathematics or Physics: some medical courses accept either Mathematics or Physics as the third A-level subject.

    d. Third Subject: while Chemistry and Biology are often mandatory, the third subject can sometimes be more flexible. Subjects like Mathematics, Physics, Psychology or even a non-Science subject may be accepted, depending on the medical school.

    e. Most medical courses require at least three A levels with grades of AAA or higher. It is important to check the specific requirements of each medical course, as they can vary slightly. Some courses will lower the offer if the pupil is attending a school with a historically deprived intake.

- **Vocational Courses:** for pupils interested in vocational futures, qualifications such as BTECs or T levels offer context-specific learning in fields like engineering, health care or digital media. These routes can lead to employment or university study, often with an emphasis on real-world applications.
- **Apprenticeships:** apprenticeships provide a blend of earning and learning, appealing to pupils eager to enter the workforce while gaining qualifications. For example, a Level 3 apprenticeship in business administration or construction can lead to a strong career and further professional development.
- **University Access Courses:** you might also highlight alternative routes to higher education for pupils whose GCSE results do not immediately meet entry requirements, such as foundation years or access courses.

Managing appeals and options

In some cases, pupils or parents may question the accuracy of results – and this is a growing trend affecting more pupils every year. Teachers and parents are finding an increasing need to appeal a result. If you think this applies to one of your pupils you should raise this with your head of department as soon as possible. Have a past paper and past grades from practice examinations for that pupil to hand in for evidence, but the first step will be for your head of department to request the paper. You should be ready to explain the appeals process, including deadlines for lodging appeals and the potential outcomes. While managing expectations, it is important to reassure pupils that there is a possibility of retaking examinations where appropriate. Your school can also work proactively to ensure pupils are aware of resit opportunities and any support that it can offer.

Positive engagement with parents and pupils

Results day is as much about celebrating success as it is about addressing concerns. Taking time to acknowledge pupils' efforts and achievements – regardless of the grades attained – fosters a positive atmosphere. For instance, a pupil achieving a Grade 5 in Mathematics after struggling throughout the year deserves recognition for their perseverance and growth. It is important that we recognise we do not just celebrate those with high grades, or indeed only those with Grade 4 or above. Pupils who worked hard to achieve their grades deserve to be celebrated.

As their teacher, you are often the first point of contact for parents seeking advice, and clear communication is crucial. For example, discussing the benefits of exploring multiple options can help families feel more in control. Statements like, "This is just the beginning of your journey, and there are so many paths to success", can be incredibly reassuring, but only if you have to hand over further information about those pathways. Seek to make yourself knowledgeable about such pathways and collate links to such further information so that you can distribute them easily. One quick way is to convert them into QR codes so that pupils and parents can quickly scan them and jump to a reliable source of information that has been curate by you and your department colleagues personally.

Whilst it is not mandatory to attend GCSE results day, it is seen as a sign of a strong commitment from you to the school and community. If you want to access autonomy and play a part in decision-making, then attending events like these and supporting the community will stand out to middle and senior leaders in the school and mark you as someone who wants to play an active role in the development of the school community.

A-Level results day

This section approaches the smaller, but more serious nature of A-level results day, which enables pupils to access post-18 work and education. It will talk about the clearing process; what pupils can do if they have better or worse results than predicted and alternative industry-based routes into sectors. There will be a range of scenarios and example advice set out so that teachers can review what they can do depending on the permutations of the results.

Supporting pupils on A-level results day

A-level results day can be an emotional rollercoaster for pupils. Some are elated, having achieved the grades they need for their chosen university or career path. Others face disappointment, uncertainty, or difficult decisions about their next steps. As a teacher, it is vital to be adaptable and supportive, helping pupils navigate this pivotal moment with clarity and confidence. Pupils will experience a wide range of emotions, from joy and relief to shock and despair. Being a steady and empathetic presence is crucial. A pupil who has just realised their grades fall short of their expectations may be overwhelmed, while another with unexpected success might suddenly feel daunted by new opportunities. Your ability to listen, guide and encourage will make a lasting difference.

Each of your pupils will have a plan for what to do if they get the results they need. They should also have a plan on what to do if they do not get the results they need – but they will likely need help clarifying if their plan is the right one. Often, the answer will be to get in touch with clearing.

Clearing

Clearing is a process in the UK UCAS application system that allows applicants who have not received an offer from a university, or who have changed their mind about their courses, to find available places at universities and colleges.

It typically begins in July and runs until September, once A-level results are released. Applicants can apply through Clearing if their exam results do not meet the conditions of their offers, or if they did not receive any offers. To use Clearing, applicants must have their UCAS Clearing number, which is provided after they receive their results. They can then search for courses with vacancies, contact universities directly, and make new applications. It is an opportunity for applicants to secure a place on a course, even after the main application cycle has closed.

Each pupil is unique

Each pupil is unique, and you should learn from the experience of other teachers who might have met some scenarios before. Here are some scenarios to help frame your ideas about how to respond to questions from your pupils following their results.

Kate's story

Kate had her heart set on studying Law and French at University X, needing BBC to secure her place. However, she received BCC and is devastated. The teacher advised Kate to remain calm and offered practical advice. She was encouraged to contact the university immediately to see if they would accept her with BCC – often, universities make such offers automatically, but if she had not heard from them, she was advised to get in contact. After making the call, Kate learned that while she could not study Law and French, the university would admit her for Law alone.

The teacher then helped Kate weigh her options. She could accept the offer for Law, especially if she loved the university and the city. Alternatively, she was advised to explore other universities through clearing to find a programme that included French, perhaps in a different location. This guidance allowed Kate to make an informed decision about her future.

Abdul's story

Abdul exceeded expectations, achieving AAA when he was predicted to be ABB. Initially planning to attend a local university with a good Biology programme, Abdul now has opportunities he had not considered. The teacher advised Abdul to explore a wider range of universities, including higher-ranking institutions in the Russell Group, which he was now eligible for.

He was guided to contact these universities through clearing to see if they had places available and discuss the practicalities of attending. For example, whether he would commute or live on campus. By helping him consider both academic and logistical factors, the teacher ensured that Abdul could make the most of his achievements.

Tez's story

Tez faced significant challenges and achieved CCD, just below the BCC needed for his desired apprenticeship. This situation called for sensitive yet proactive support. The teacher advised Tez to contact the apprenticeship provider to see if they might still accept him, given his circumstances. If not, they would explore alternative apprenticeships or consider the option of applying to university next year.

Tez's resilience in achieving his grades was acknowledged, and the teacher ensured he knew his options remained open. Whether he chose to enter the workforce, pursue an apprenticeship or continue his studies, the teacher provided encouragement and practical advice.

Jacki's story

Jacki, predicted CCD, aimed to study Management at a university known for its affordable living costs. However, she received DDD and was told her grades were insufficient for a place. Jacki was understandably distraught, feeling as though she had no viable options.

In such moments, the teacher reassured Jacki that clearing offered opportunities to find alternative courses, either in management or a related field. She was also advised to consider retaking her exams to improve her grades if she had the support at home to do so. Addressing her anxiety and self-confidence was equally important, ensuring that Jacki felt equipped to face the challenges ahead when she returned to sixth form.

Supporting retakes

As you have seen in the scenarios, for some pupils, retaking their exams may be the best course of action. Offering hope during what may feel like a time of despair is not only a professional responsibility but also a human one. You should consult with the head of sixth form to ensure you understand the school's expectations for pupils retaking exams and provide accurate advice about whether they can do this with the school or have to take them elsewhere.

It is essential to present retaking as a viable path rather than a setback. For example, a pupil who narrowly missed their required grades might use the retake period to refine their understanding of the subject and strengthen their academic skills. By framing retakes as an opportunity for growth, I can help pupils regain confidence and motivation.

The role of teachers

In these moments, our role extends beyond the classroom. We become mentors, guides and sources of reassurance for pupils navigating one of the most significant transitions in their lives. By listening carefully, providing clear advice and fostering a sense of hope, we help them move forward with determination and confidence.

Getting ready for your new classes

This section is focused on the fact that most teachers go into school over the summer break and undertake some general housekeeping on their teaching space, their resources and so forth, to ensure that they are as ready as they can be for the start of term. This frees up time in September to ensure that a strong start can be made.

If you are appointed to start in September

When starting at a new school, teachers are often allocated a classroom along with a set of resources such as stationery and, in some cases, tech-based tools to support day-to-day teaching. The resources provided depend largely on the subject. As a teacher taking up a new post, you may go into school during the summer to set up your room according to your preferences and evaluate just what resources your teaching space or department provides for you. This will include organising the layout, creating displays and arranging posters, along with considering the overall setup of tables and desks. It is also a time to review the resources available to you (for example, a PE teacher will need to check equipment, whereas an English teacher will want to see what set texts are available), assess whether you need to supplement them, and perhaps write or source new planning and teaching materials.

Room setup

Your school may have specific guidelines regarding the layout of tables or the teacher's desk. It is crucial to be aware of these directives and follow them to ensure compliance with school policy. However, most are fairly supportive if you have a particular layout that you know has been successful for you. You should be aware that some schools will insist on tables being in rows, but this is not true for all schools.

When setting up your classroom, there will be many aesthetic and functional considerations to bear in mind. For example, you may need to decide on the colours of display boards and posters you wish to use. Are the colours to your liking, or would you prefer to make changes? Will you need a small desk for resources beside your main desk, and how will you arrange the tables to facilitate the type of teaching you plan to deliver? Consider whether each class or year group will have a separate display board and think about the typography and clarity of the lettering you will use to indicate the focus of each display. Additionally, it is worth reflecting on whether you will incorporate keywords on the walls and whether this aligns with school guidance. You will also have the responsibility of deciding how many keyword sections to include and what style of posters best supports the learning you aim to foster.

Layout

The arrangement of desks in the classroom has a direct impact on how you will teach. Whether you opt for rows of desks, small tables or another arrangement, the way pupils are positioned will influence classroom dynamics. Rows, where pupils face forward, can provide better sightlines for you to monitor engagement and participation. This setup also allows for easier classroom management, as you can quickly observe which pupils are focused and which may need additional support. However, you must consider how this configuration might limit your ability to incorporate group work effectively into your lessons. If you prefer a more interactive style of teaching, small tables of four to six pupils might be a better option. This arrangement facilitates group work, collaborative discussions, and activities such as group competitions. It can also support the development of social skills and independence among pupils. However, many find that grouped tables are challenging and prefer to have the room in rows and move the tables to groups for specific activities.

Walls and displays

Many schools have different policies regarding the use of walls as tools for learning. If your school has display boards, consider their location carefully and think about how visible they will be from various areas of the classroom. For instance, it might not be wise to place keywords or exam techniques on a board that is not easily visible to all pupils. Additionally, it is important to strike a balance between vital information, such as rules and guidelines, and promotional material. As much as you want them to, pupils often decline to read anything related to rules and guidelines and will only use displays about work if it is pertinent to the task at hand.

Movement around the room

It is essential that you have easy access to all areas of the classroom, as well as to each pupil, so that you can provide support when needed. A smooth flow of movement around the room is necessary to ensure a safe and efficient learning environment. Consider how you will create clear walking paths that allow pupils to enter and exit the room with minimal disruption and also enable you to circulate the room readily to check work or answer questions. Leave your teaching space in a state that you want to enter the space in September and think "this is the perfect place for me to teach". That is why you give up your precious summer holiday time to get your room just right – it is about controlling the environment so that you benefit from your own work.

And finally...

This section revisits the key themes of the book: being evidence-informed, being adaptive, focused on wellbeing, looking to ensure future employability, retention and finally mobility of a teaching career. It will bring together an overview of the cycle of schools in England and position the key points of the year with a view to setting out how a teacher can be assertive and still autonomous within the centralised structure of England's education system.

Good luck and welcome to your new school!

As we reach the conclusion of this book, it is important to revisit the key themes that have been woven throughout the monthly sections: being evidence-informed, adaptive, focused on wellbeing, ensuring future employability and embracing the mobility of a teaching career. These themes are not just abstract concepts but practical tools that can help you navigate the dynamic and sometimes challenging landscape of teaching in secondary schools in England.

Being evidence-informed is at the heart of effective teaching. Throughout the year, whether you are planning for new classes in September, using data to inform your teaching in December, or conducting intervention investigations in July, grounding your practice in solid evidence ensures that your decisions are based on what works. This approach not only enhances your teaching but also builds your credibility and autonomy within the school. By staying current with research and best practices, you can confidently adapt centralised planning to better meet the needs of your students and regain the autonomy and opportunity for creativity that some teachers today complain they have lost.

Adaptability is another crucial theme. The educational landscape is constantly evolving, and as a teacher, you must be flexible and responsive. From establishing behaviour management strategies in October to incorporating creative teaching methods in February, being adaptable allows you to meet the diverse needs of your students and create a dynamic learning environment. This flexibility also extends to your professional development. By engaging in self-directed CPD and seeking out opportunities to enhance your skills, you can stay ahead of the curve and remain a valuable asset to your school. But remember, your school is focused on your school's metrics, not you. Do not only focus on school metrics – develop yourself as well so you can move to other schools with different metrics to enhance.

Focusing on wellbeing is essential for both you and your pupils. Teaching can be demanding, and it is important to prioritise your own health and happiness. Whether it is managing stress during the busy exam season in May or maintaining a healthy work-life balance in July, taking care of yourself ensures that you can be the best teacher possible. This focus on wellbeing also extends to your students. By creating a supportive and inclusive classroom environment, you can help them thrive both academically and personally.

Ensuring future employability is a theme that runs throughout the book. The teaching profession is dynamic, and it is important to be proactive in managing your career. From building confidence in your professionalism in March to using gained time for professional development in June, taking ownership of your career trajectory ensures that you are prepared for whatever the future holds. This includes being open to new opportunities and continuously seeking ways to enhance your skills and knowledge.

Finally, embracing the mobility of a teaching career is essential in today's educational landscape. Schools and MATs can change rapidly, and being able to move fluidly between different institutions is a valuable skill – especially if your head teacher changes or your school is brokered to a new MAT. Whether it is navigating the challenges of a new school in January or preparing for a new academic year in August, being mobile and adaptable ensures that you can thrive in any educational setting. This mobility also allows you to bring fresh perspectives and innovative ideas to each new role, enhancing your impact as an educator.

In conclusion, the cycle of schools in England presents both challenges and opportunities. By being evidence-informed, adaptable, focused on wellbeing, ensuring future employability and embracing the mobility of a teaching career, you can navigate this landscape with confidence and autonomy. Remember, you have the power to shape your career and make a lasting impact on your pupils. Stay curious, stay committed and continue to grow as a professional. Your journey as a teacher is a dynamic and rewarding one, and we hope this book has provided you with the tools and inspiration to thrive in your career.

Index

absences 110, 111, 112
academic attainment 68, 75
academic curriculum 45; *see also* curriculum
activities: end-of-term 111; extra-curricular 14, 25, 34, 72, 101–103; group-based 72; language-based 71; physical 64, 101, 103, 111
adaptation 54–55; curriculum 109; differentiation to 57; dividing 54–55; in-lesson 54; pre-lesson 53, 54, 56
adaptive learning 53–57; *see also* learning
adaptive teaching 53–57; classroom culture 56–57; differentiation to adaptation 57; diversity of learners 53–54; dividing adaptation 54–55; scaffolding/support for SEND pupils 56; *see also* teaching
adolescence 103
AfL *see* Assessment for Learning
Alan Turing Cryptography Competition 102
A-Level results day 116–118; clearing 116–117; pupils stories 117–118; role of teachers 118; supporting pupils on 116; supporting retakes 118
anxiety 30–37, 68, 76, 79, 99, 113, 118; causes of 34; new senior leaders 30–31
apprenticeships 64, 114–115, 118
assertiveness 94, 96, 97
assertive professionalism 94–97; difficult conversations 95; pre-exam conversations 94–95; professional boundaries 95–96; recognising bias 96–97; responding assertively 97; toxic colleagues 95–96; unconscious bias 96
assessment: diagnostic 28; end-of-unit 46–49; formative 27, 28, 55; integrated 47–48; objectives 7; planned 47–48; timing of 48–49; transparent goals 27; *see also* end-of-unit assessments

Assessment for Learning (AfL) 43; addressing misconceptions 27; Chartered College of Teaching 29, 30; clear learning objectives 27–28; diagnostic assessment 28; Education Endowment Foundation (EEF) 29; embedding formative assessment 27, 28; importance in classroom 26–27; modern feedback methods 28–29; not one-size-fits-all approach 30; strategies for effective 27–28; summative assessment planning 28; in teaching 26–30; transparent assessment goals 27; utilising resources 29; whole-class feedback 27
atmosphere 14, 79, 104, 115
attainment 4, 15, 95; academic 68, 75; impact on 68
augmented reality (AR) 64
awkward conversations 94

behaviour: clear/precise/rapid communication 24; consistency rules 13; constructive feedback 22; contacting parents about 16–17; demonstrating strengths 25–26; early 5–6; to establish authority 12–26; good 13, 23, 111; high-quality 18; leadership in schools 19; for learning 13, 17; liaising with colleagues 19; low-level 15; management policy 2, 12–26, 111, 121; meeting pupils 5–6; new ideas 23–24; new organisation challenge 22–23; personal learning community 20–22; policy 60, 62; professional development 24–25; reflective teachers 17; relationships and 18–19; rewards 14–15; sanctions 14–15; school-led 13–14; school pastoral system 15–16; substantive difficulties 16; values-led approaches 19–20
bias: acknowledge 97; recognising 96–97; unconscious 96

Bourdieu, Pierre 4, 73
bullying 24, 45, 76
Burgundy Book 37–38, 59, 85, 100
burnout 32, 54, 83, 99

career: alternative 84; development 82–85; goals 83; objectives 83; personalised 82; planning 85; progression 109–110; second 82; trajectory 83; and uncertain future 83–84
centralised planning 7, 10, 50, 69, 86–93, 104, 121; *see also* planning
Chartered College of Teaching 26, 29, 30, 105, 108, 109
Chartered Teacher Status (CTeach) 108, 109
Chromebooks 65
classes/classroom: AfL importance in 26–27; culture 56–57; dynamics 107, 120; high expectations 56–57; importance of AfL in 26–27; of inclusivity 56–57; management 105, 120; planning for new 5–6; productive environment 69; trust/connection outside 73–74; *see also* new classes
Clayton's DEAL model 90–91
clear communication 24; *see also* communication
co-constructed instructional coaching 22
cognitive overload 23, 79
collaborative reflection 92–93
colleagues: advice from experienced 70; building rapport with 9–11; collaborative 21, 43; confrontational 94; liaising with 19, 26, 69; meeting with 24; observing 105; poor culture for 24; toxic 95–96
communication: clear/precise/rapid 24; confidence in 84; effective 99; electronic 24; good 84; honest 38; official channels 96; one-way 16; oral 20; school 16; skills 41, 84; software 16–17; unhelpful 24; via app 16; written 24; *see also* conversations; interactions
confidence: building as teacher 80, 81; in creativity 72; cultivating 80–81; in professionalism 80–82; and revision strategies 86–87
confrontational conversations 94
consistency rules 13
constructive dialogue 97
constructive feedback 22, 36, 42, 81; *see also* feedback
content: examination 6–7, 71; feedback on 41; high-level 54; learning 56; new 63, 68; in options evenings 78; ressure to deliver 70; subject 78; substantive 20
Continuing Professional Development (CPD) 70, 82–85, 105, 110, 121–122
conversations: confrontational 94; difficult 95; evidence-based 94; pre-exam 94–95; *see also* communication; interactions

corporate style school 2–3; *see also* school
creative teaching 69–72; approaches 71–72; building confidence 72; group work 72; language-based activities 71; music/media 71–72; role play 71; strategies for 70–71; *see also* teaching
culture: classroom 56–57; of continuous learning 29; of cooperation 26; corporate 2; new 23; old 22–23; parental 32; poor 24; school 5, 22, 96; of silent working 18; toxic 36
curriculum: academic 45; adaptations 109; availability of 2; expensively produced 8; pastoral 45; pre-existing design 7–9; and stress 33; technology across 64–65

data: analysis 7, 51; from assessments 51–52; drawing conclusions from 52; drops 46–47, 50, 52; mock exams 59; question-by-question 59; rationale for 50–51; tracking 47
Department for Education (DfE) in England 1, 31
designated safeguarding lead (DSL) 61, 62
diagnostic assessment 28; *see also* assessment
differentiated learning 55, 57; *see also* learning
difficult conversations 95; negative realities 95; positive praise 95; *see also* conversations
diplomacy exit 37
discrimination 56, 94
Dubey, R. 9
Duke of Edinburgh scheme 106

early career teacher 3, 31, 35, 92
education: education 2, 3, 53; effective environment 19, 26; higher 14, 39–40, 42, 115; personal 14, 83; physical 23, 43, 48, 51, 64, 68; principle equity 55; religious 77; scope of 107; social 14, 83; special 55
Education Endowment Foundation (EEF) 26, 29
emotional language 24
employability 3, 8, 72; boosting through mobility 3; fluid 1; future 1, 108, 121–122; through mobility 3
end-of-term activities 111
end-of-unit assessments 46–49; integrated assessment 47–48; planned assessment 47–48; timing of assessments 48; tracking data 47; *see also* assessment
English as Additional Language (EAL) 51
environment: education effective 19, 26; feedback-rich 29; productive 69; safe and structured 62–63
epistemic curiosity 8–9, 64, 70

Equality Act 18–19
equity in education principle 55
evidence: -based conversations 94; grounding reflection in 90
evidence-informed 20, 24, 33, 121–122; investigations 104; knowledge 96; objections 33; practice 8, 50, 52, 86, 104–105; teachers 9, 80, 88
exams/examinations: analyse performance 7; assessment objectives 7; choosing/preparing questions 58; content 6–7; criteria 6–7; learning of 6–7; mock 42–43, 44; performance analysis 7; practice 87; prior learning of 6–7; reteach misconceptions 7
excessive stress 36; *see also* stress
existing staff 32
expectations 68–69; academic 62; for behaviour management 5; consistent 14; cultural 39; high 10, 32, 53, 55–57; school-specific 69
experienced teacher 4, 34; *see also* teacher
extra-curricular activities 14, 25, 34, 72, 101–103; adolescence and 103; encouraging lifelong habits 102; importance of physical activity 103; in secondary schools 101–102; subject specialisms and 102–103; *see also* activities

face-to-face meeting 24, 98
feedback 41–42; codes 29; constructive 22, 36, 42, 81; modern methods 28–29; -rich environment 29; seeking 81; whole-class 26, 27, 28–29
food parcels 75–76
formative assessment 27, 28, 55; *see also* assessment
form tutor 44–46
Free School Meals 76
free schools 1–2

gained time/re-timetabling 101, 104–105, 108, 110, 122; collaborating with HOD 104; enhancing subject knowledge 104–105; evidence-informed practice 8, 50, 52, 86, 104–105; maximising 108, 110; new timetable 105; observing colleagues 105; refining practice 105; showcasing pupils' work 104
General Certificate in Secondary Education (GCSE) 2, 6, 26–30, 43, 51, 52, 64–65, 77–78, 99, 112; guidance on pathways 114–115; managing appeals and options 115; positive engagement 115–116; results day 113–116; revision lessons 86; significance of 114
Gibbs' Reflective Cycle 90, 91
good behaviour 13, 23, 111; *see also* behaviour

Gothic literature 21
Griffiths, T. L. 9
grounding reflection 90
group-based activities 72

Heads of School 19
higher education 14, 39–40, 42, 115; *see also* education
honest communication 38; *see also* communication
hooks 79
Human Resources (HR) 16–17, 23, 37–38, 60, 97
hunger 76

If it's important, then I'm curious: Increasing perceived usefulness stimulates curiosity (Dubey, Griffiths and Lombrozo) 9
imposter syndrome 77, 80, 81
Industrial Revolution 107
Information and Communication Technology (ICT) 16, 23
in-lesson adaptation 54; *see also* adaptation
instructional coaching: co-constructed 22; prescriptive 22
integrated assessment 47–48; *see also* assessment
interactions: effectiveness 98; face-to-face 98; influencing 96; in options evenings 78; with parents 24; personal 98; poor 14; positive 68; social 32, 110; with subject communities 80; *see also* communication
International Baccalaureate 114
intervention investigation 108–110; career progression 109–110; maximising gained time 108, 110; professional recognition 109–110; research in practice 108–109; structured framework for 109
interventions: and actions 52; effective 58–59
interviews: coaching pupils for 41; mock 41–42; Oxbridge 41; PSRB 41

Keeping Children Safe in Education 19
Key Stage 3 7, 28, 30, 77–78, 105
Kolb's Experiential Learning Cycle 90, 91–92

language-based activities 71; *see also* activities
leadership: equitable 24; good 57; middle 19; poor 36; schools 13, 19, 80, 83; senior 31
learners: diversity of 53–54; equipping with tools 107; pupil as 7; reluctant 10
learning: adaptive 53–57; collaborative reflection 92–93; evaluating sequences

of 88–93; experience 25, 26; grounding reflection 90; high-quality 24; hunger impact on 76; objectives align with creativity 71; reflection as lever for progress 93; reflective frameworks 90
lifelong habits 101, 102, 103
local authority school 1; *see also* school
Lombrozo, T. 9
long-standing relationships 33

meeting: with colleagues 24; face-to-face 24, 98; online 98; pupils 5–6
middle leadership (ML) 19; *see also* leadership
miscommunications 32–33; *see also* communication
mock examinations 42–43, 57–59; choosing/preparing questions 58; managing time 58; managing workload 59; post-examination tasks 59; purpose of 58–59; revision support 58
modern feedback methods: feedback codes 29; feedback-rich environment 29; maximising impact 28–29; reducing workload 28–29; whole-class feedback 28–29; *see also* feedback
motivation 13, 36, 56–57, 68, 87–88, 118
multi-academy trust (MAT) 2–3, 9, 15, 19, 23, 50, 56, 57, 82, 97, 109
multitudinous pupil 9–10; *see also* pupil
music/media 71–72

National Foundation for Educational Research 4
National Professional Qualifications (NPQs) 84
new classes 119–120; displays 120; layout 120; movement around room 120; room setup 119; walls 120; *see also* classes/classroom
new ideas 23–24
new organisation, challenges 22–23
nudge style tactics 14

Office for Standards in Education, Children's Services and Skills (OFSTED) 104
one-size-fits-all approach 30, 88
one-way communications 16; *see also* communication
online meetings 98; *see also* meeting
online reporting mechanisms 12, 18
options evenings 77–80; activities and engagement 79–80; content 78; hooks 79; interaction 78; practical concerns 79, 80; preparing for 78–79; professional conduct 80; right atmosphere 79; room 79; stall and presentation 78–79
oral communication 20; *see also* communication
out-of-class teaching 105–107; *see also* teaching
Oxbridge 39–42; courses 41; interviews 41

parents: celebration/support 113; positive engagement 115–116; pre-exam conversations with 94–95; and stress 32–33
parents' evenings 44–46, 98–100; adapting year groups 99; honest/productive relationships 99; online formats 98; time management 99–100; traditional 98
passive-aggressive bullying 24
pastoral care 72–75
pastoral curriculum 45; *see also* curriculum
pastoral system 15–16
pedagogical approaches 2, 33, 108–109
pedagogical practice 88–93
pedagogy: curriculum and 33; instructional 70; subject-specific 90
physical activity 64, 101, 103, 111; *see also* activities
physical education 23, 43, 48, 51, 64, 68
planned assessment 47–48; *see also* assessment
planning: actions 52; career 85; centralised 7, 10, 50, 69, 86–93, 104, 121; data drops 50; drawing conclusions from data 52; for holidays 111; identifying patterns 51; interventions 52; measuring progress 51–52; for new classes 5–6; pre-existing 2, 8–9, 21, 69, 108; rationale for data 50–51; self 8; summative assessment 28; using data 50–52
Point, Evidence and Explain (PEE) 56
positive relationships 16, 44, 87
post-examination issues 104
post-examination tasks 59
PowerPoints 10, 33, 58, 70, 79
precise communication 24; *see also* communication
pre-exam conversations 94–95; *see also* communication
pre-existing planning 2, 8–9, 21, 69, 108; *see also* planning
pre-lesson adaptation 53, 54, 56; *see also* adaptation
prescriptive instructional coaching 22
primary school 2; *see also* school
Professional, Statutory and Regulatory Bodies (PSRBs) 41
professional boundaries 95–96; official communication channels 96; safe spaces 96; set clear boundaries 95
professional conduct, options evenings 80
professional development: active participation in 24–25; opportunities 24; sessions 25

professionalism 81; assertive 94–97; confidence in 80–82
professional learning communities (PLCs) 20–22, 24, 25
professional pigeonholing 97
professional recognition 109–110
professional record 97
professional relationships 9, 19, 21, 26, 37, 97
PSRB see Professional, Statutory and Regulatory Bodies
pupil(s): building rapport with 9–11; celebration/support 113; choices 78; coaching for interviews 41; greeting 68; multitudinous 9–10; personal data 6; positive engagement 115–116; as potential customer 78; poverty 75, 76; prepare thoroughly 71; preparing for university applications 39–40; progress measurement 51–52; relationship b/w teacher and 67; for self-study 88; showcasing work of 104; understand 71
Pupil Premium initiative 76

rapid communication 24; see also communication
rapport building 9–11, 67, 77–78; confidence 10–11; with new pupils/colleagues 10–11; preparation 10
rapport rebuilding: impact on attainment 68; post-holidays 67–69; strained relationships 67–68
recognising bias 96–97; judgements tied 97; professional pigeonholing 97; stereotyping 96; see also bias
re-establishing routines 62
reflective frameworks 90
reflective teachers 17
relationships: and behaviour management 18–19; honest 99; long-standing 33; positive 16, 44, 87; productive 99; professional 9, 19, 21, 26, 37, 97; rebuilding tips 68–69; strained 67–68; strengthening 107
religious education 77; see also education
resignations 4, 35, 37–38, 59–60, 85, 100
reteach misconceptions 7
revision strategies 86–88; adaptive 88; confidence through understanding 86–87; creative 88; exam practice 87; GCSE revision lessons 86; knowing pupils 87
revision support, mock examinations 58
rewards 14–15
role play 71
room: movement around 120; options evenings 79; setup 119
routines, re-establishing 62

safeguarding 61–63, 76; potential issues 61–62; re-establishing routines 62; safe and structured environment 62–63
sales pitch 78
sanctions 14–15, 17
school: communications 16; corporate style 2–3; duty 75–76; formal policy 15; free 1–2; funding in England 1–2; holiday 67; informal policy 15; leadership in 19; -led behaviour management policies 13–14; local authority 1; marketisation of 1; new 121–122; pastoral system 15–16; rely on electronic systems 6; zero tolerance 15; see also primary school; secondary school
school trips 72–75, 105–107; abroad 72–73; boosting career 74; building trust/connection 73–74; enriching learning 107; fundraising initiatives 75; logistics and safety 73; make difference 73; safety 106–107; scope of education 107; ski 72–75; socio-economic challenges 75–76; strengthening relationships 107; success 106–107; supporting all pupils 74–75; taking leap 74; types of 106–107
Science, Technology, Engineering and Maths (STEM) 106, 112
secondary schools 2, 5, 8, 13–14, 19, 21, 53, 65; dominant model for 2; extracurricular activities in 101–102; teachers 47
secondary teacher 4, 20, 36, 64, 72, 106
self-assessment 88
self-efficacy 56–57
self-planning 8
SEND coordinator (SENDCO) 46
senior leaders 30–31
senior leadership team (SLT) 19
Shakespeare 47, 89
sixth form 114, 118
skiing trip 72–75; see also school trips
social construction 17
social constructivist teaching 24
social interaction 32, 110
social usefulness 9
socio-economic challenges 75–76
special educational needs and disabilities (SEND) 48, 53, 55, 57; scaffolding 56; support for 56
stereotyping 96
strained relationships 67–68; see also relationships
strengths, demonstrating 25–26
stress 30–37; causes of 34; changing schools 37; and curriculum 33; excessive 36; integration 31–32; lack of 35; long-term 82; moving schools can induce 30; new senior leaders 30–31; parents and 32–33; and pedagogy 33; realistic boundaries 34; scrutiny of teaching

standards 31; strategies for managing 34–36; symptoms of 35; unreasonable 36
subject: communities 82; content 78; specialisms 102–103; specific pedagogy 90
summative assessment 27, 28; *see also* assessment
summer holiday 110–111, 120

teacher: capability 31; early career 3, 31, 35, 92; effectiveness 52; evidence-informed 9, 80; experienced 4, 34; miscommunications with parents 33; practical strategies for 76; reflective 17; relationship b/w managers and 25; relationship b/w pupil and 67; secondary 4, 20, 36, 64, 72, 106; training 3, 15–16; well qualified 3
Teacher Tapp 2, 3
teaching: Assessment for Learning (AfL) in 26–30; creative 69–72; mock exams 44; out-of-class 105–107; reflection models in 92; reflection phase of 89–90; social constructivist 24; standards scrutiny 31; use of technology in 63–66
technological integration 65
technology: across curriculum 64–65; beyond interactive whiteboard 64; in teaching 63–66
tech-savvy future 65–66
telephone calls: negative 17; positive 17
time management 58, 99–100
timetable, new 105
toxic: colleagues 95–96; line managers 84–85
transparent assessment goals 27
transposable habitus 1, 4, 73

UCAS: about pupils 43; applications 39–44; changes 42; clearing 116–117; coaching pupils for interviews 41; collaborate 43–44; cultivating passion 40; for dentistry 41–42; guiding pupils 42; knowledge for university degrees 40; for medicine 41–42; mock exams 44; mock interviews and feedback 41–42; moderate 43–44; personal statements 42; predicted grades 42; preparing pupils 39–40; replicate conditions 43; supporting Oxbridge applicants 40–41
uncertain future 83–84; *see also* career
unconscious bias 96; *see also* bias
university access courses 115
University Technical Colleges (UTCs) 1–2
unknown future school 3–4
unreasonable stress 36; *see also* stress
US Civil Rights Movement 28

values-led approaches 19–20
virtual reality (VR) 64
vocational courses 114–115

wellbeing: addressing absences 112; behaviour management 111; dietary adjustments 111; maintaining 111; and personal satisfaction 110–112; planning for holidays 111; summer holidays 110–111; timetable changes 111–112
well-qualified teachers 3; *see also* teacher
WhatsApp 24, 32–33
whiteboard 8, 63, 64
whole-class feedback 26, 27, 28–29; *see also* feedback
workload management 59
written communication 24

year groups 4, 98–99, 119

For Product Safety Concerns and Information please contact our EU representative GPSR@taylorandfrancis.com
Taylor & Francis Verlag GmbH, Kaufingerstraße 24, 80331 München, Germany

www.ingramcontent.com/pod-product-compliance
Lightning Source LLC
Chambersburg PA
CBHW082101230426
43670CB00017B/2920